Welcome, Parents!

I am thrilled to present this coloring book, a delightful journey for your child into the world of creativity and imagination. Designed with joy and learning in mind, this book offers a progressive approach to drawing, ensuring an enriching experience for your little artist.

Our coloring book starts with simple shapes and easy-to-follow designs, perfect for young children just beginning to explore their artistic skills. As your child flips through the pages, they'll discover that the drawings gradually become more detailed and sophisticated, gently challenging their abilities and encouraging their growth.

This step-by-step progression helps build confidence and fine motor skills, making the process fun and rewarding. Each page is a new adventure, filled with opportunities for your child to express their unique creativity.

We hope this coloring book brings endless smiles, laughter, and colorful moments to your home.

Happy coloring!

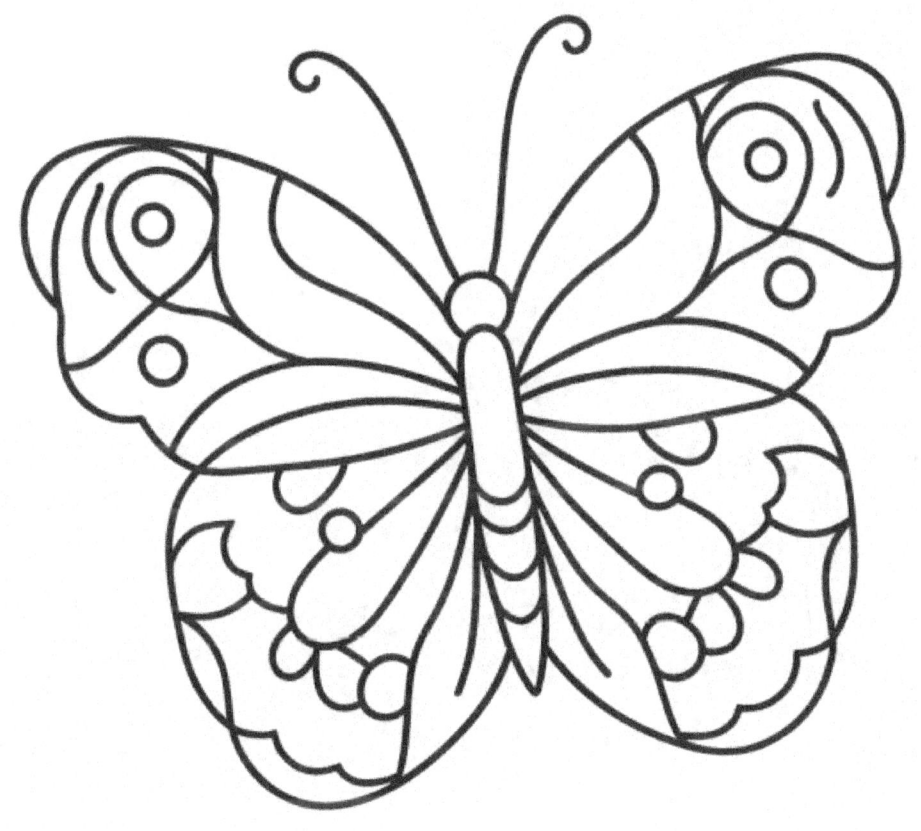

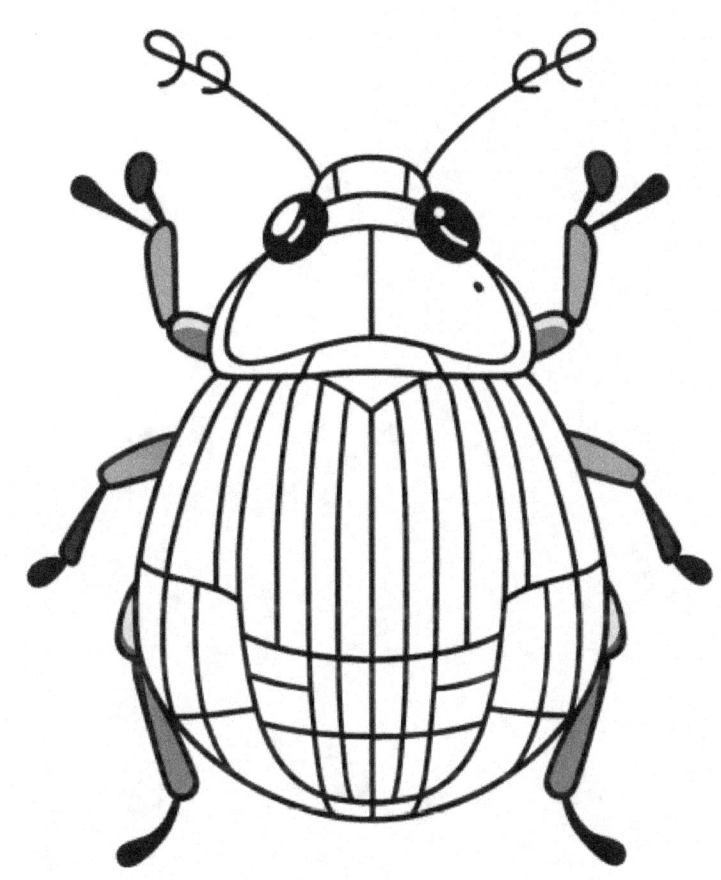

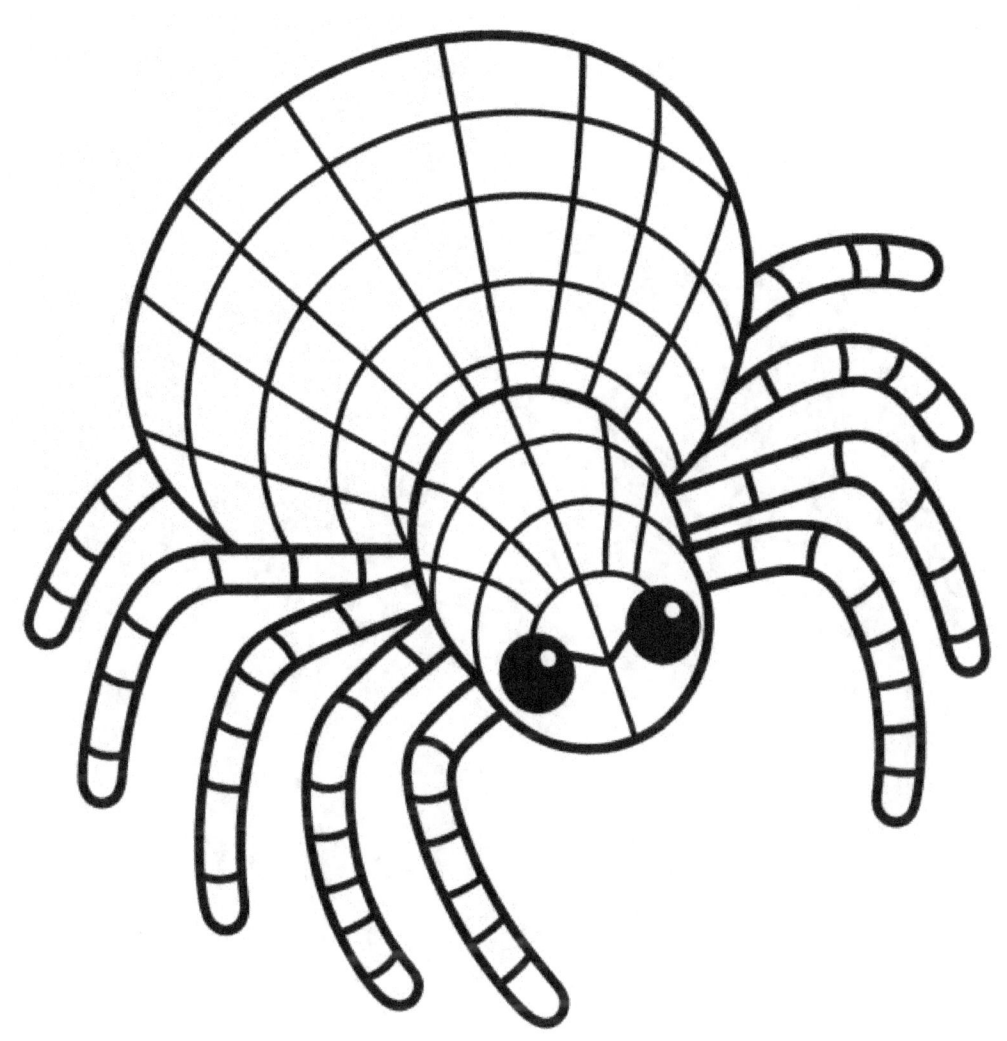

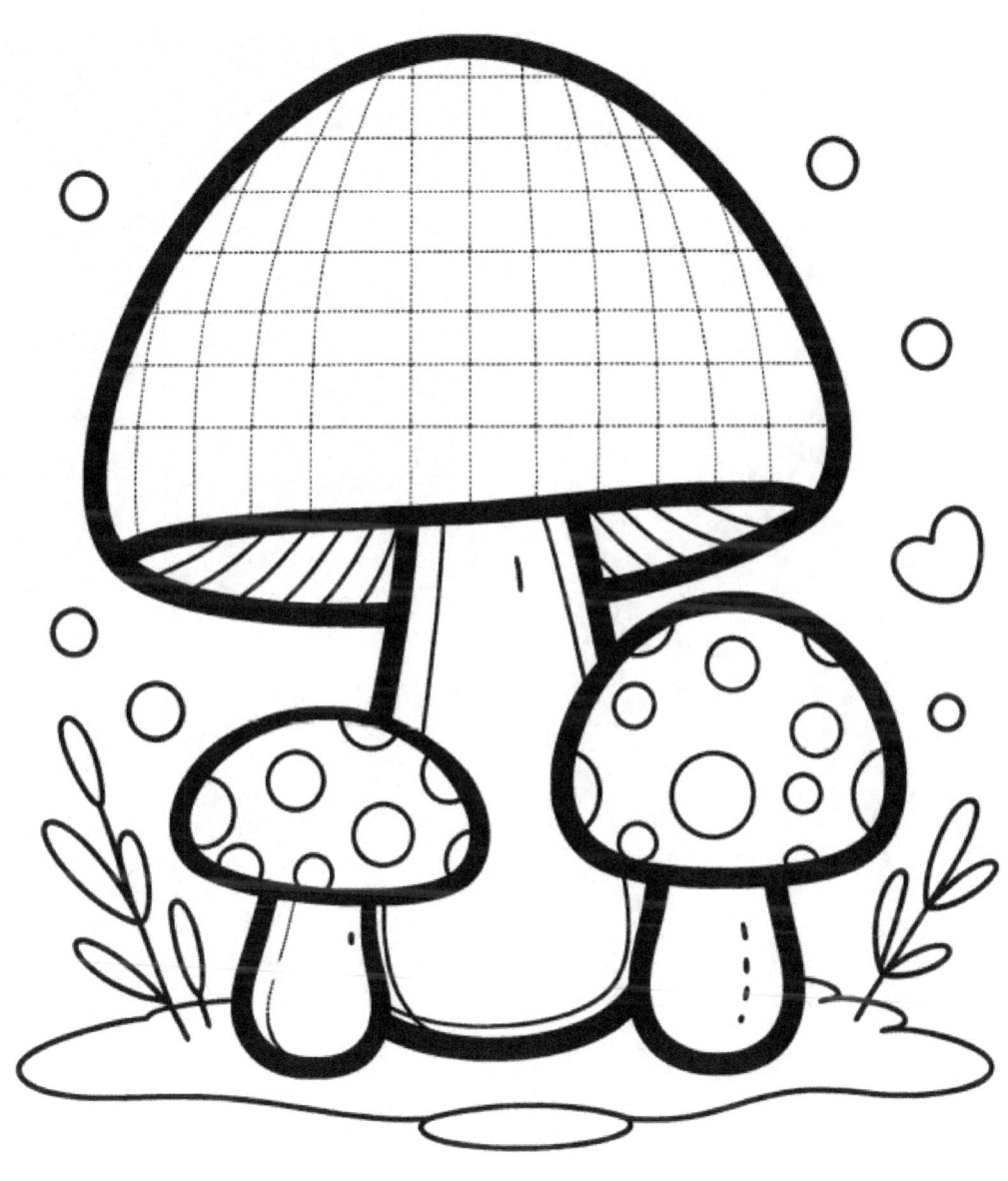

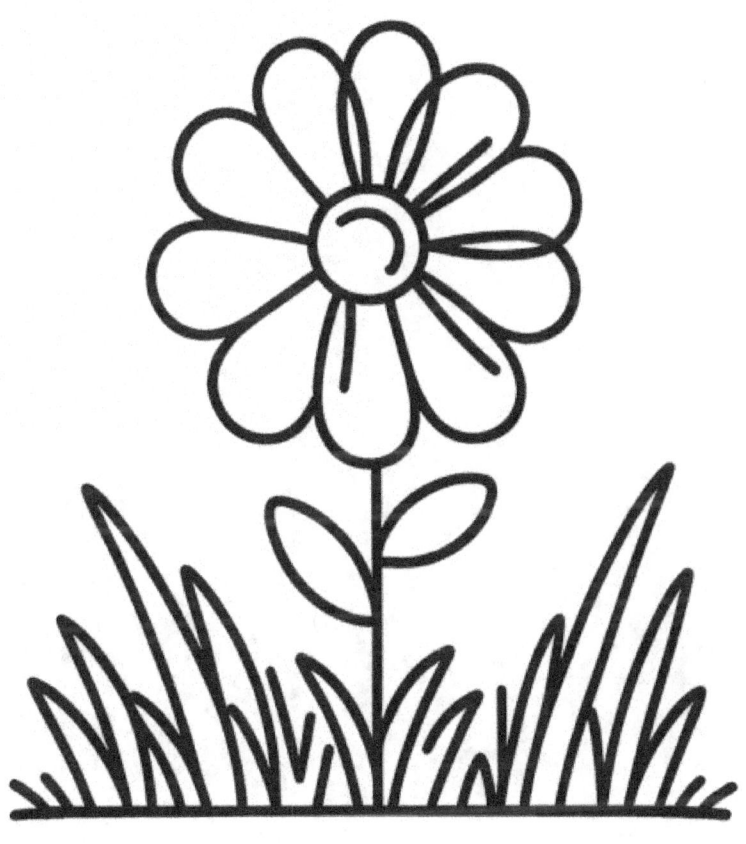

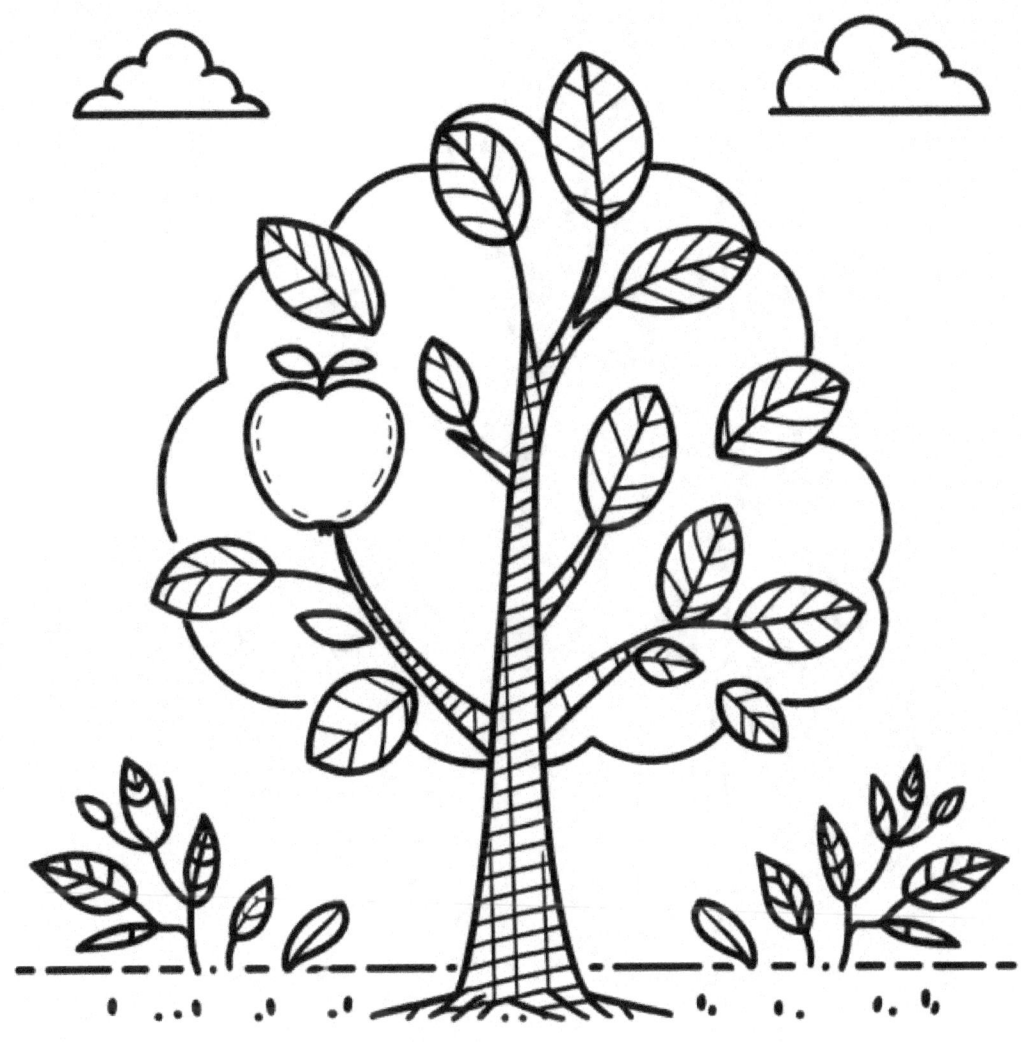

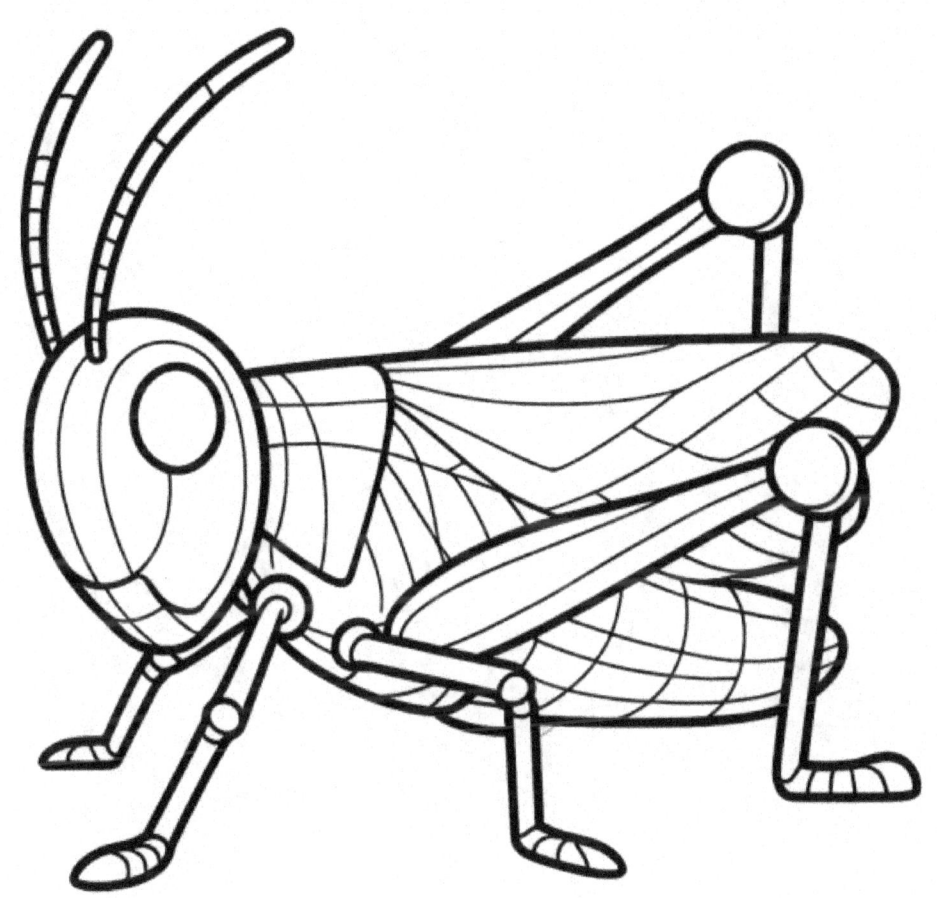

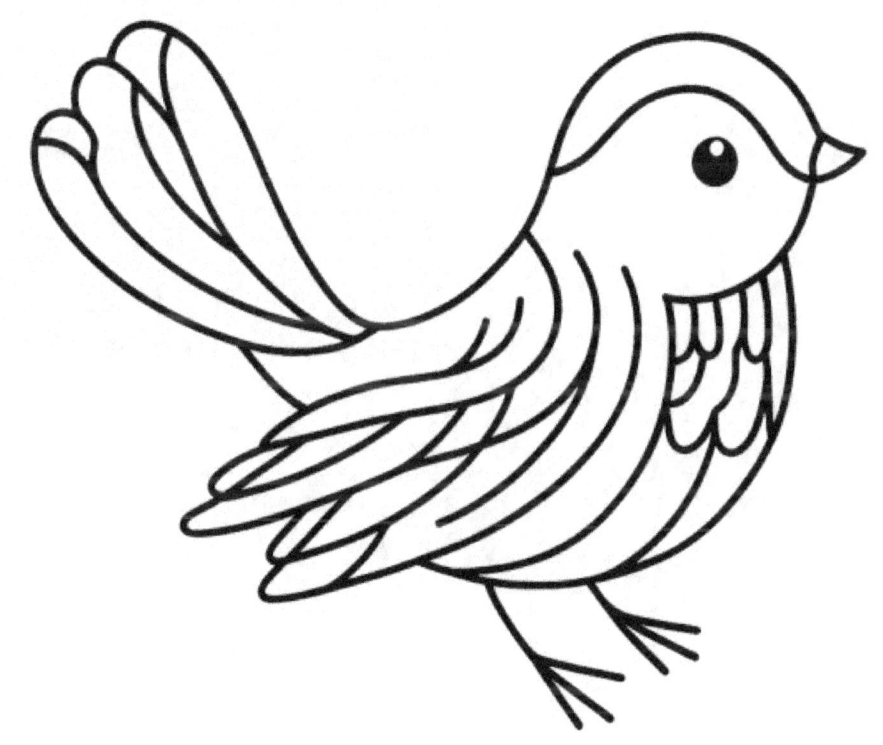

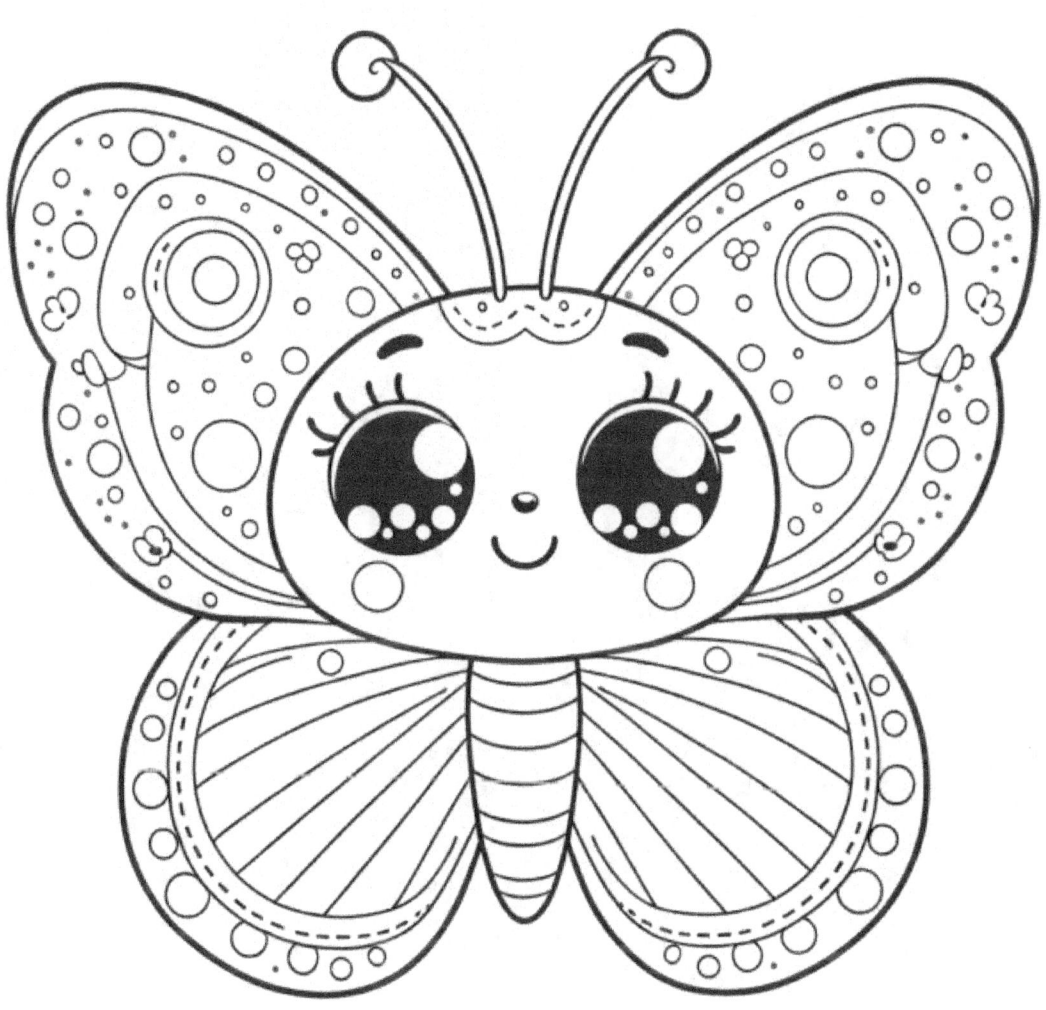

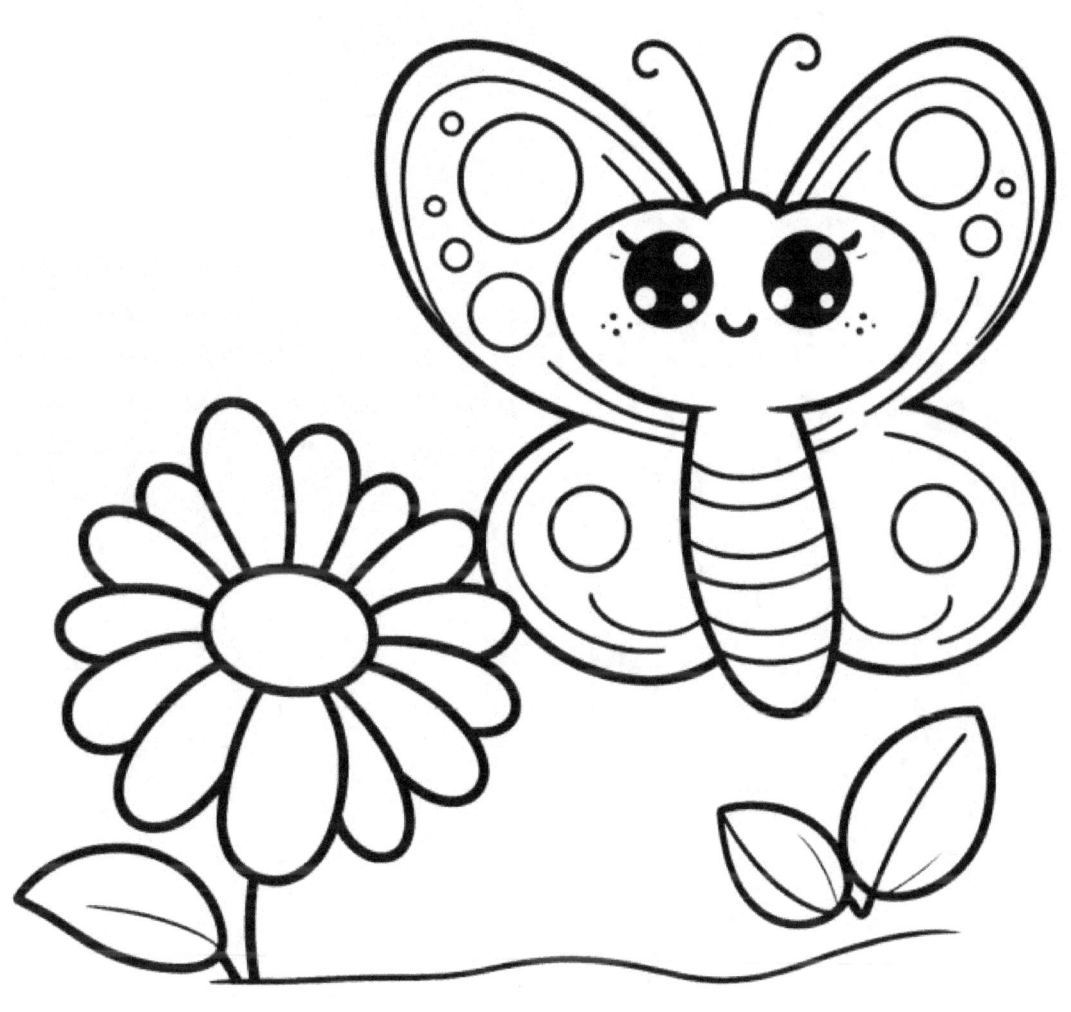

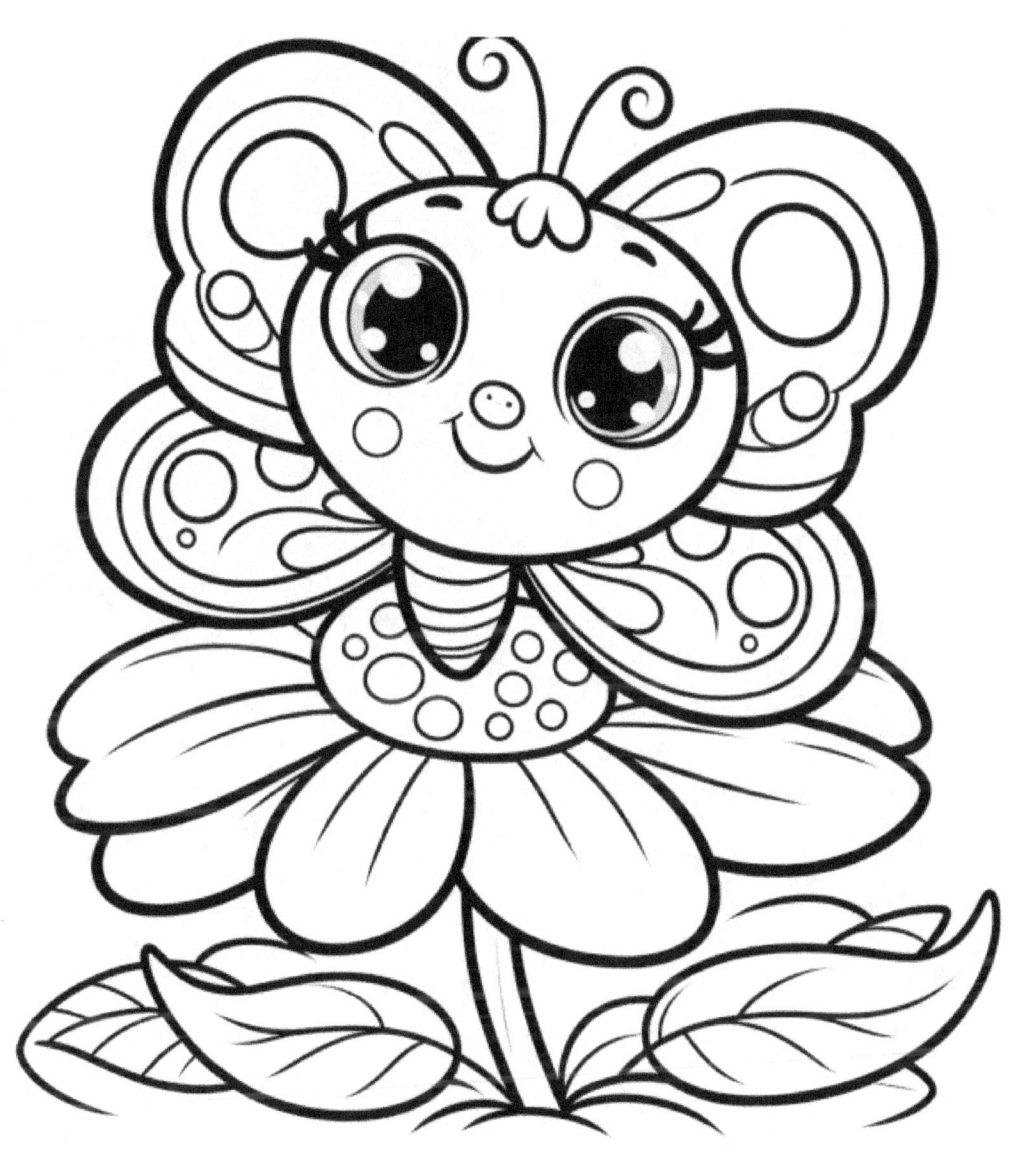

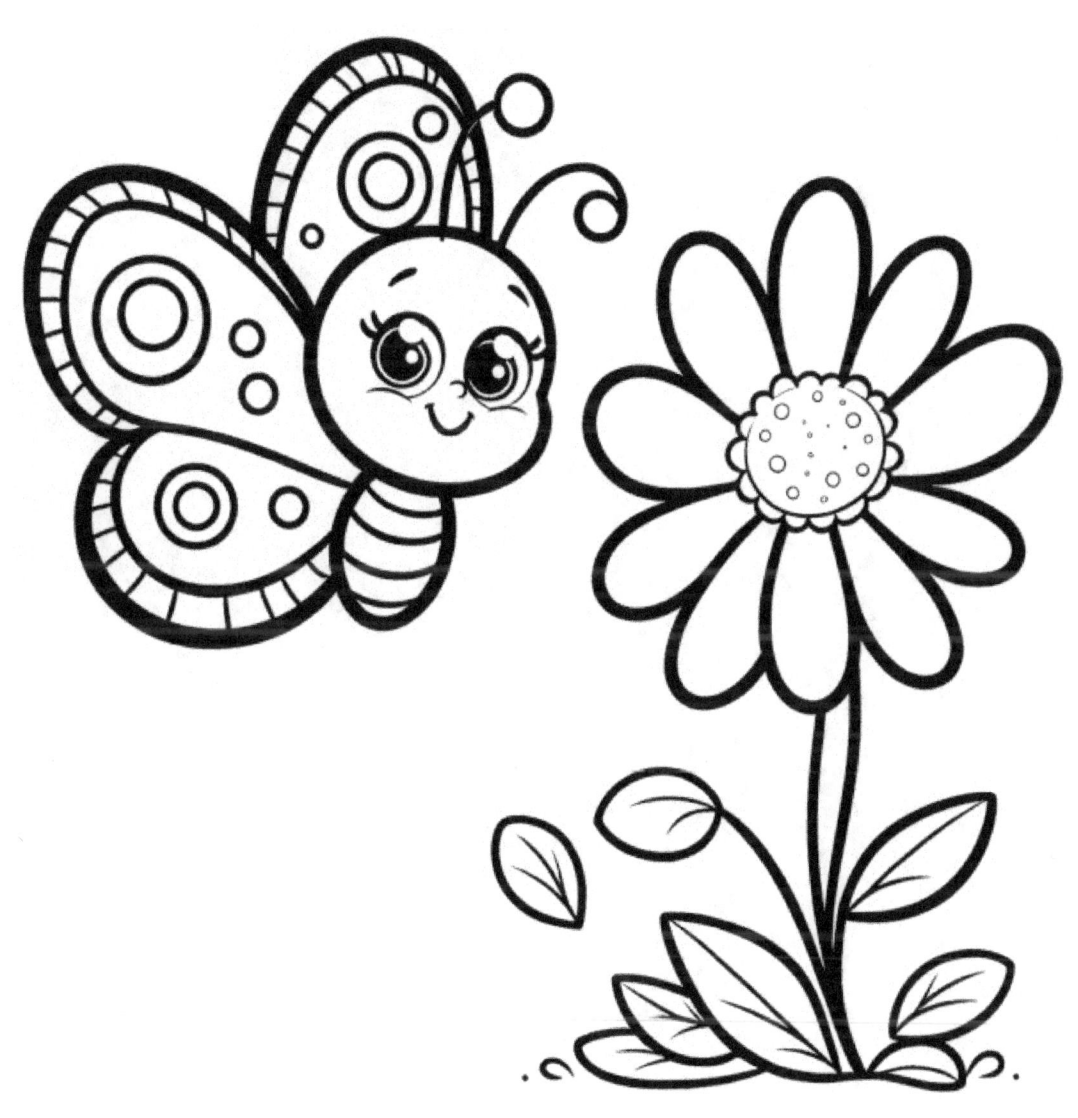

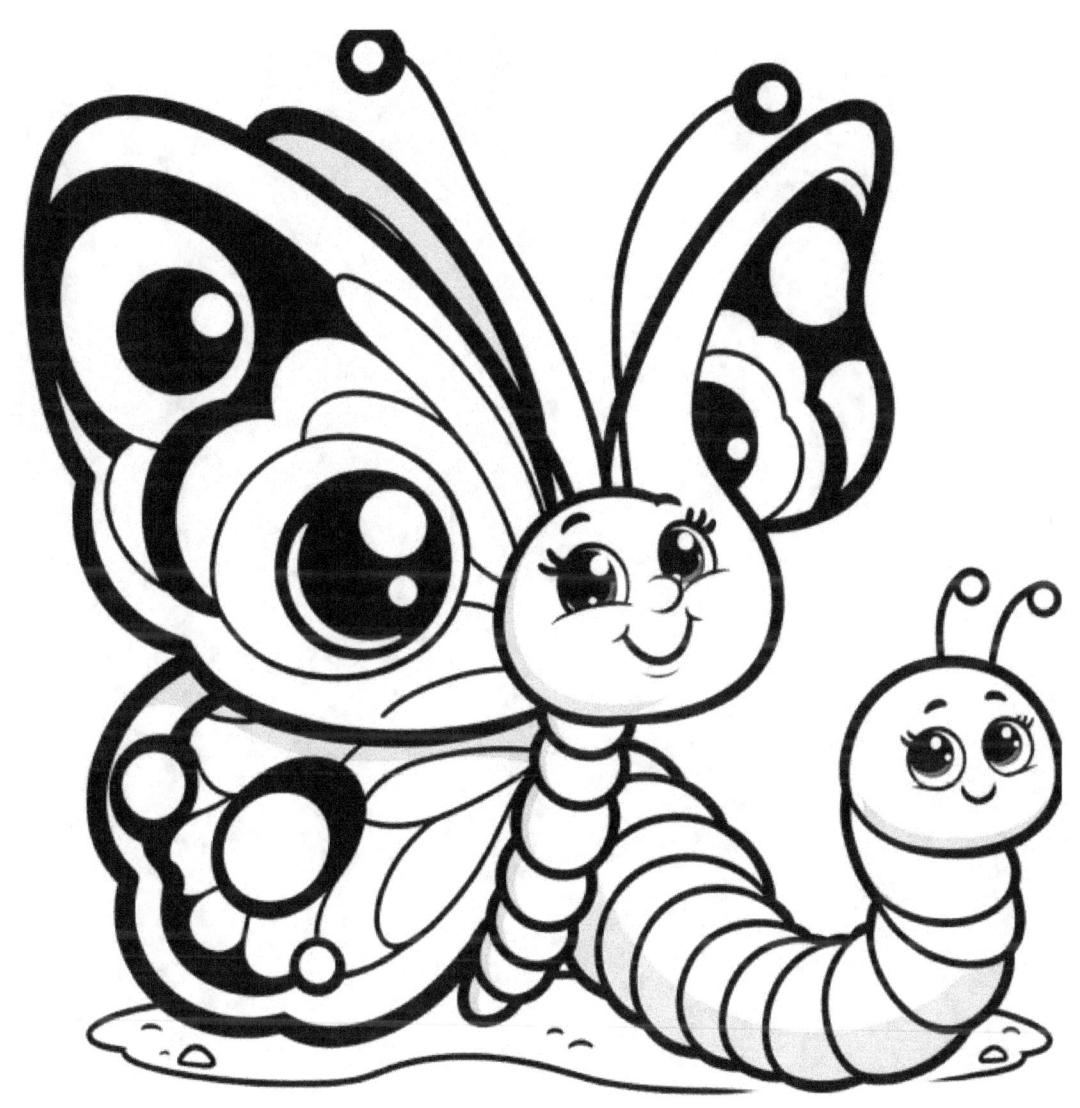

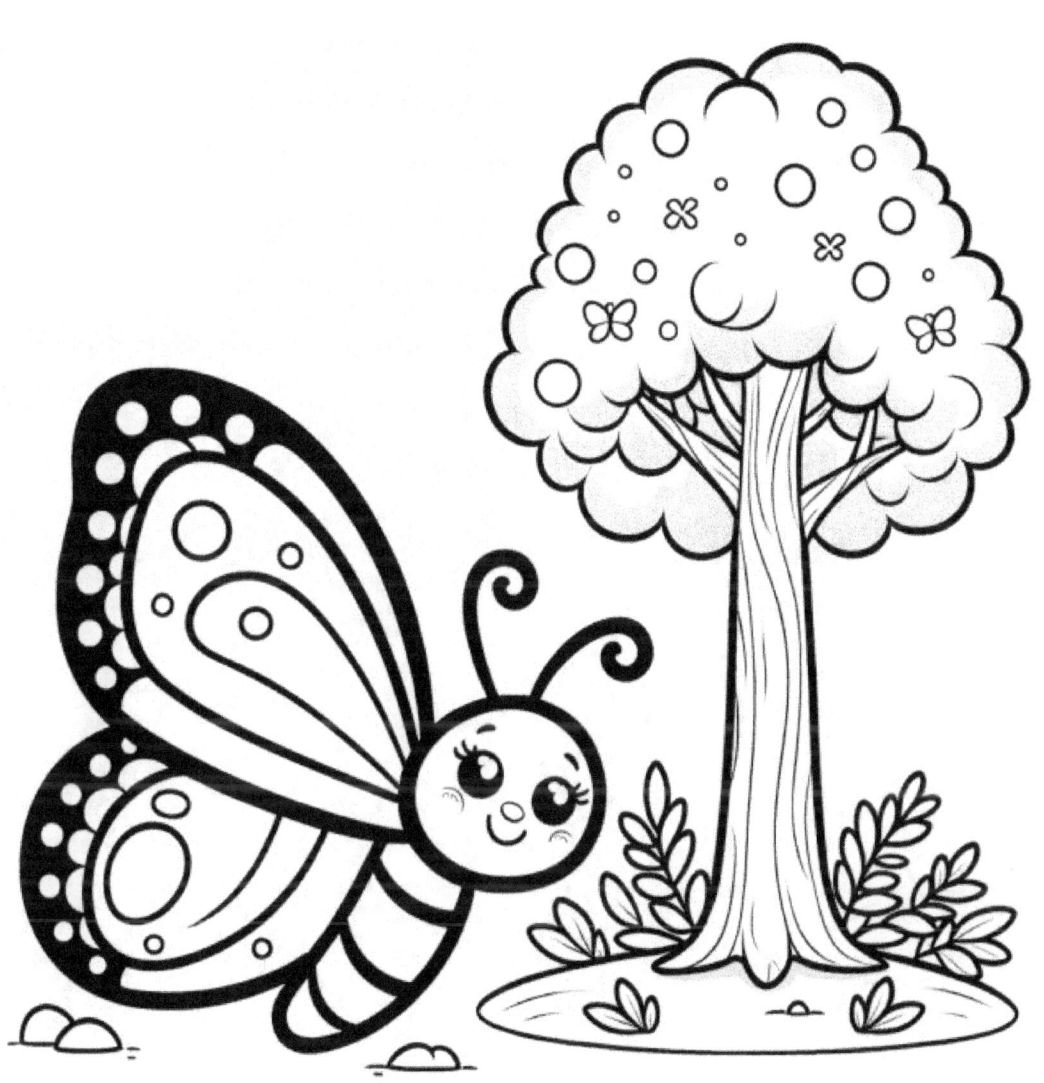

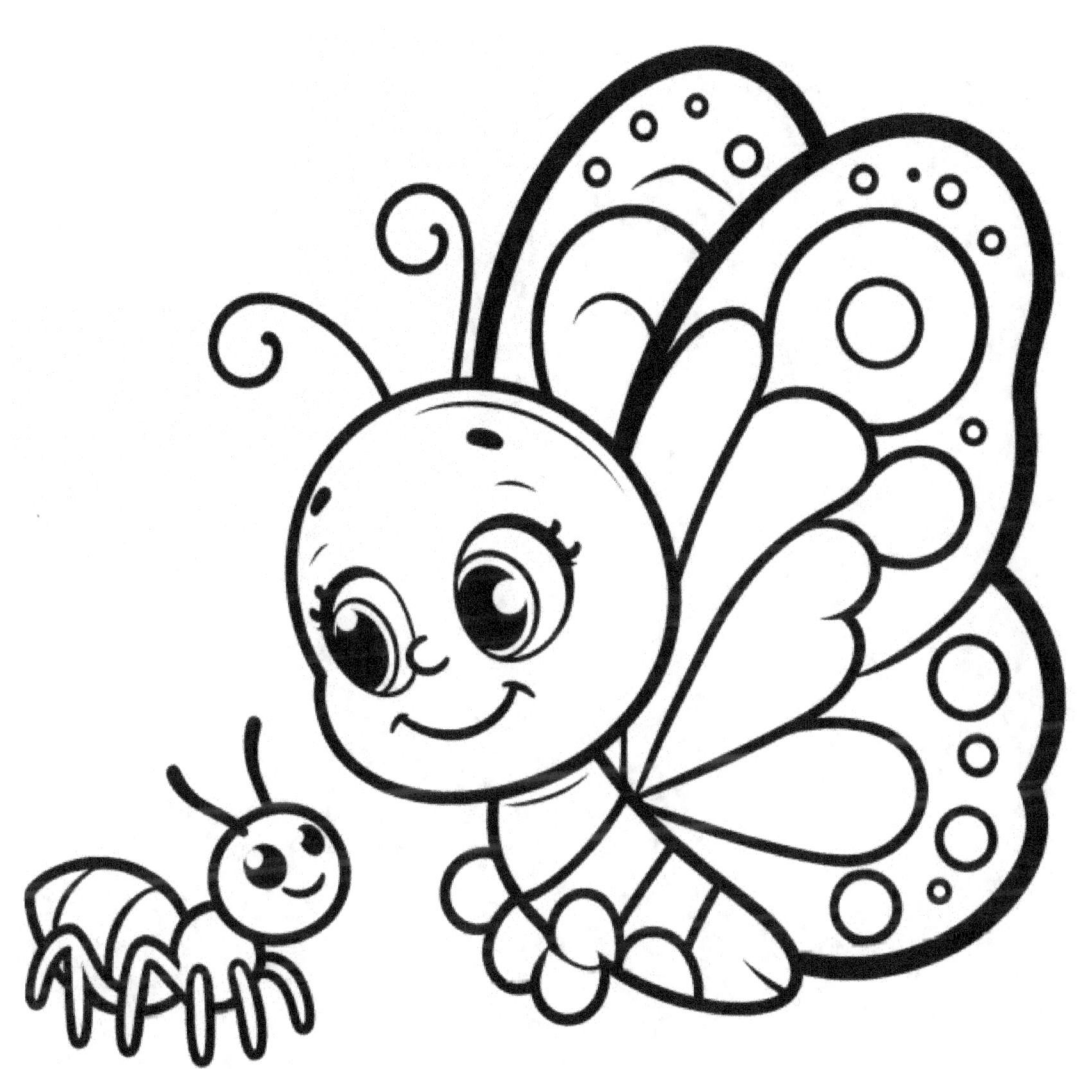

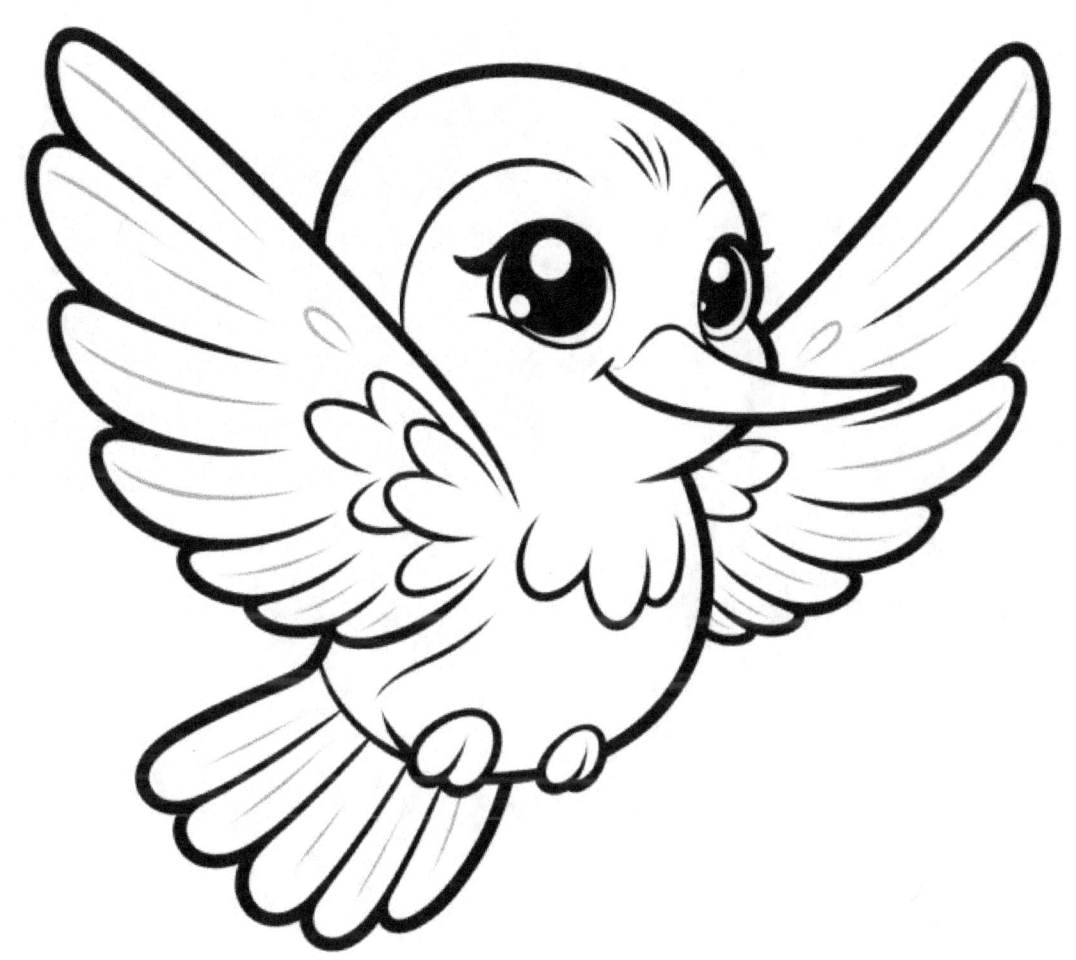

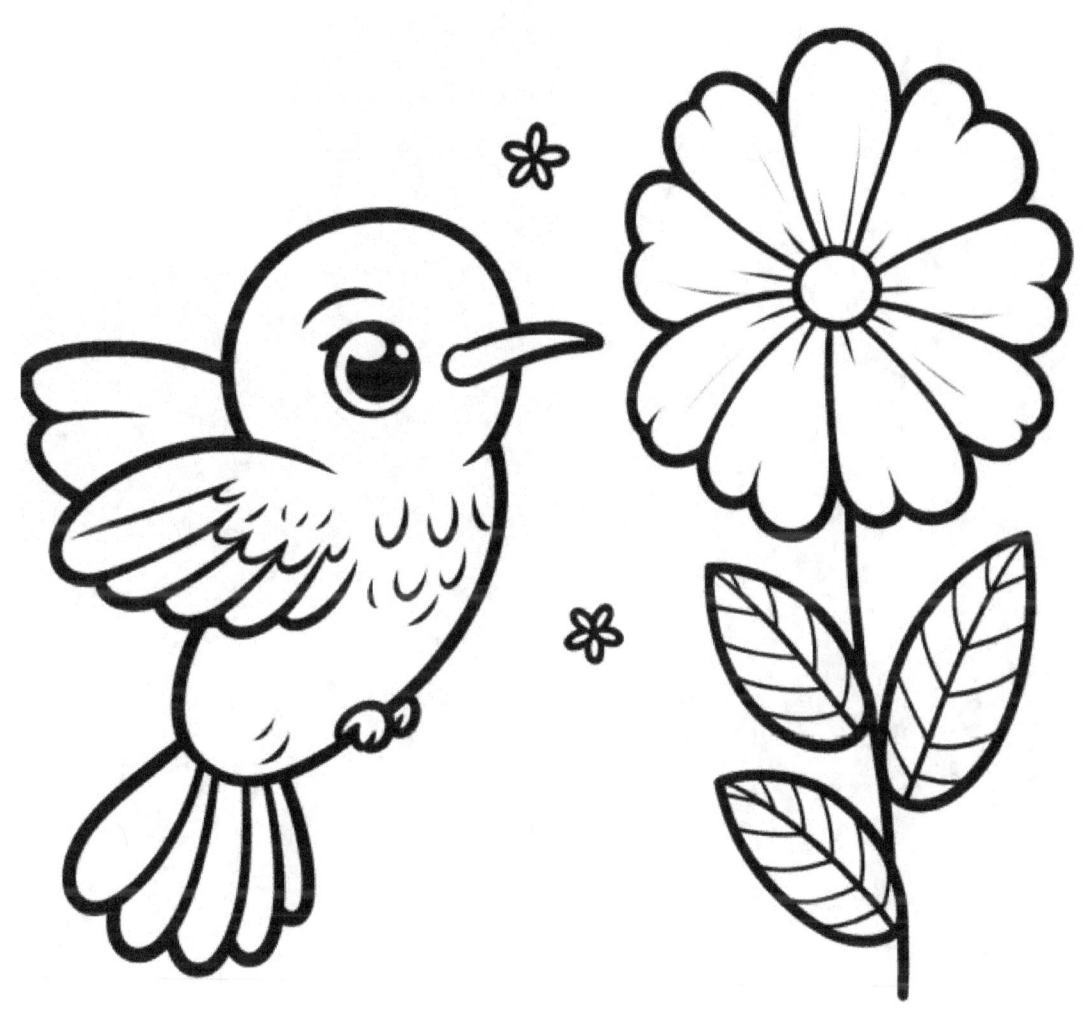

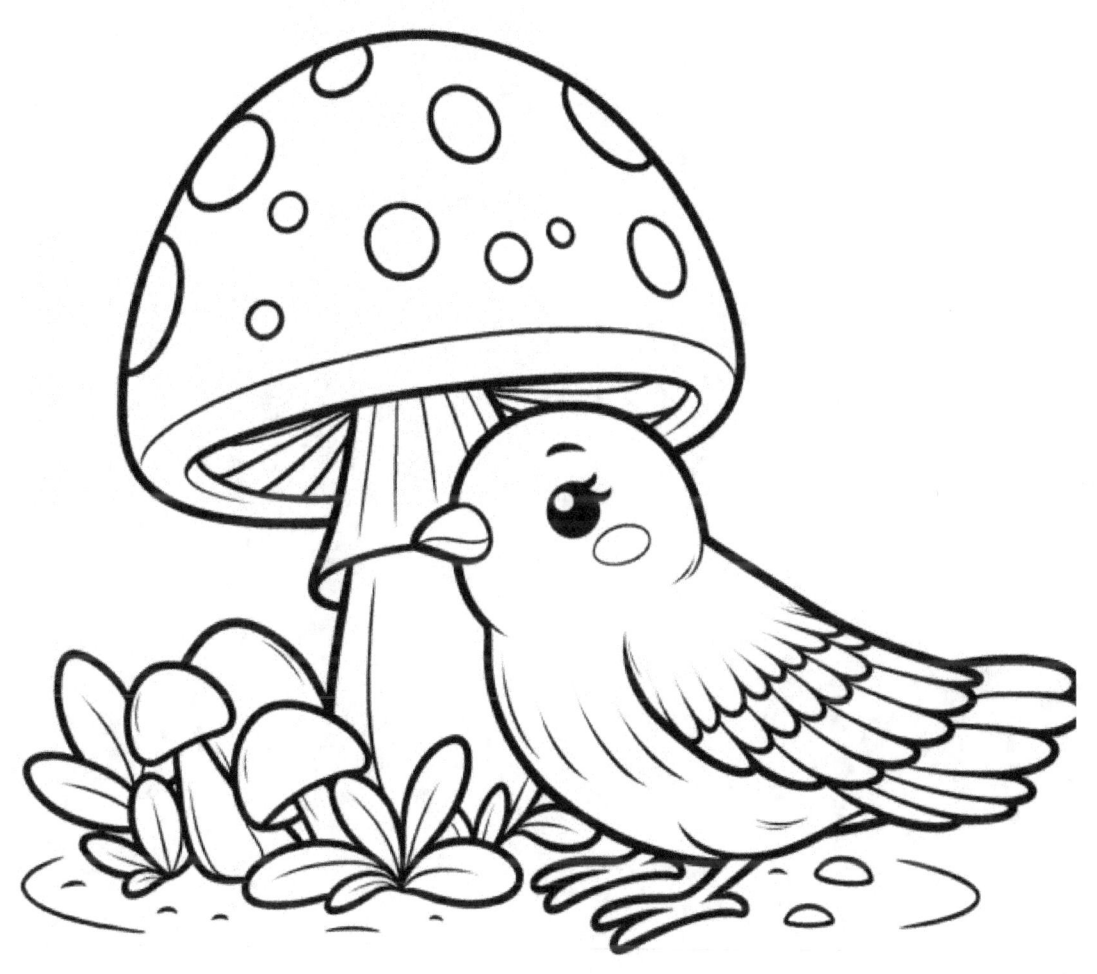

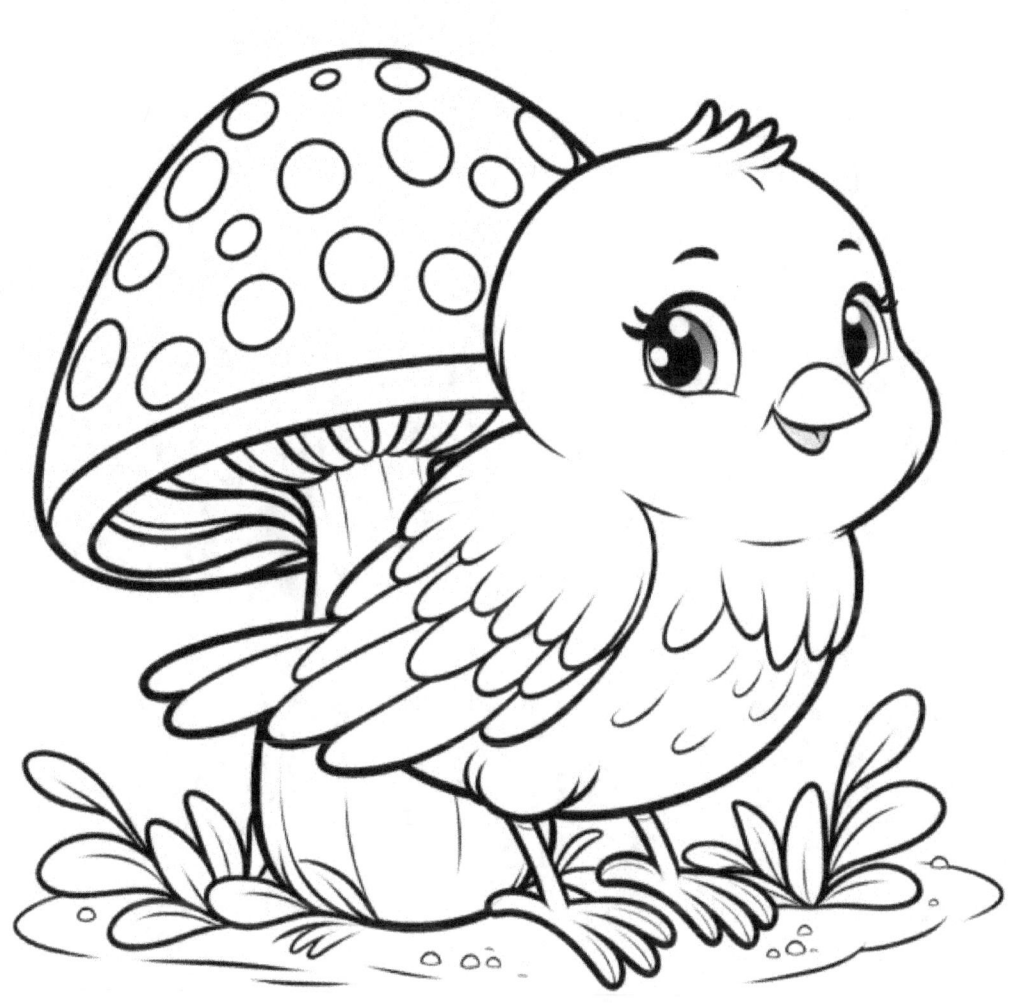

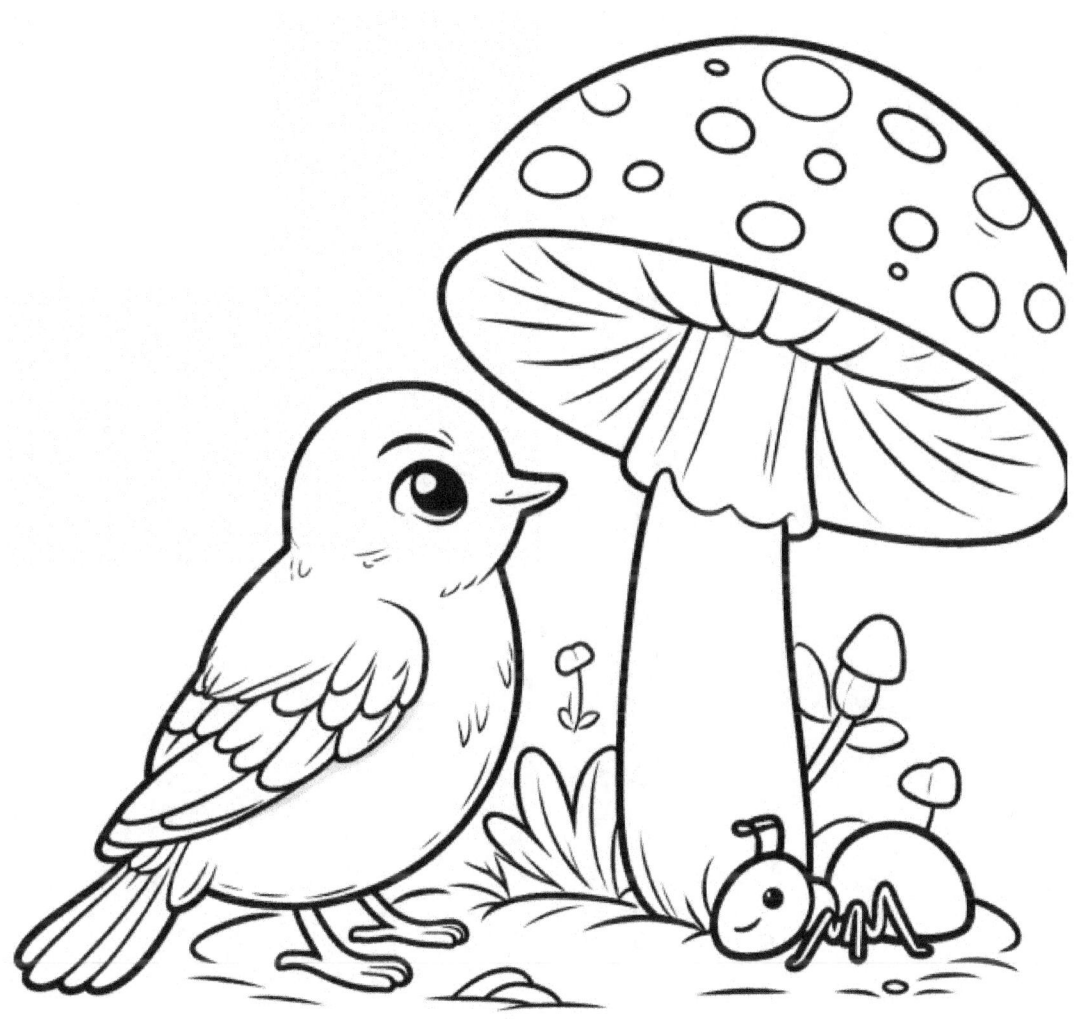

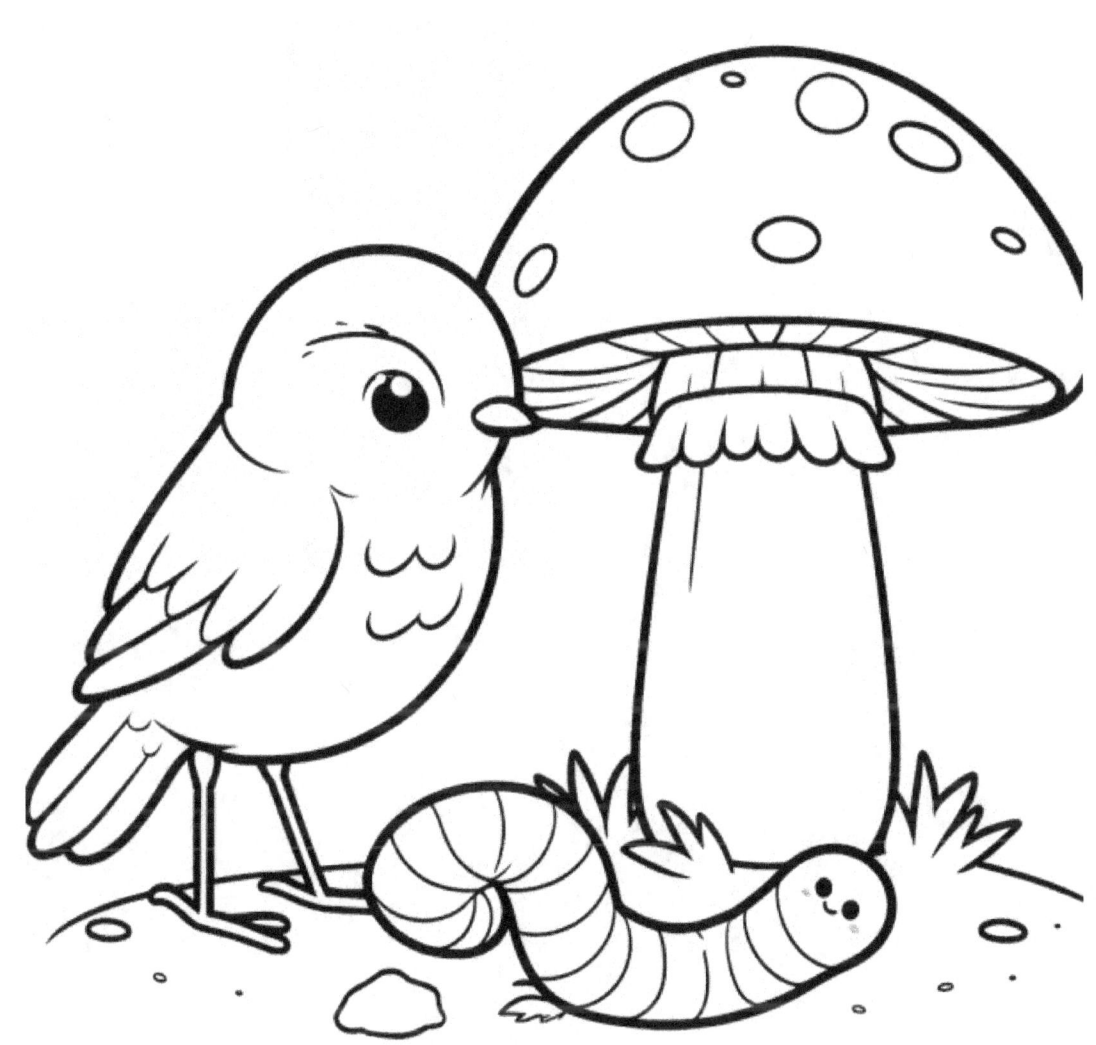

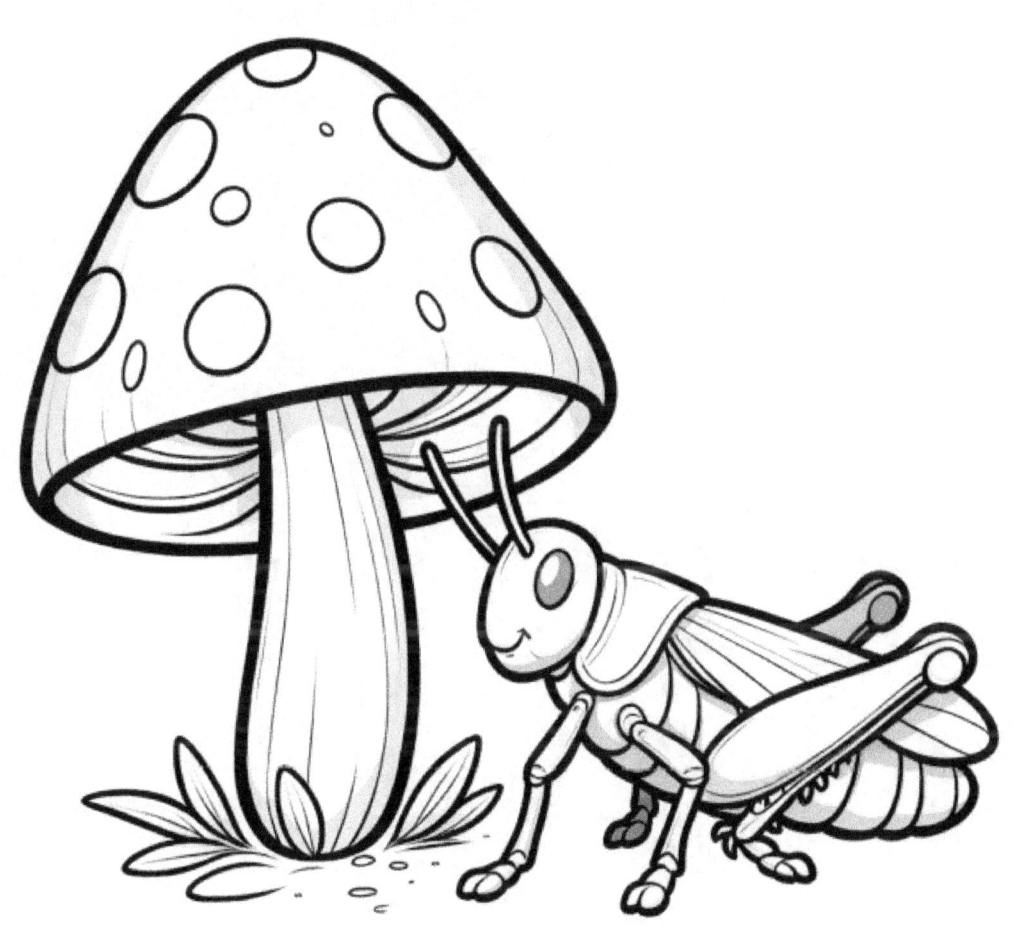

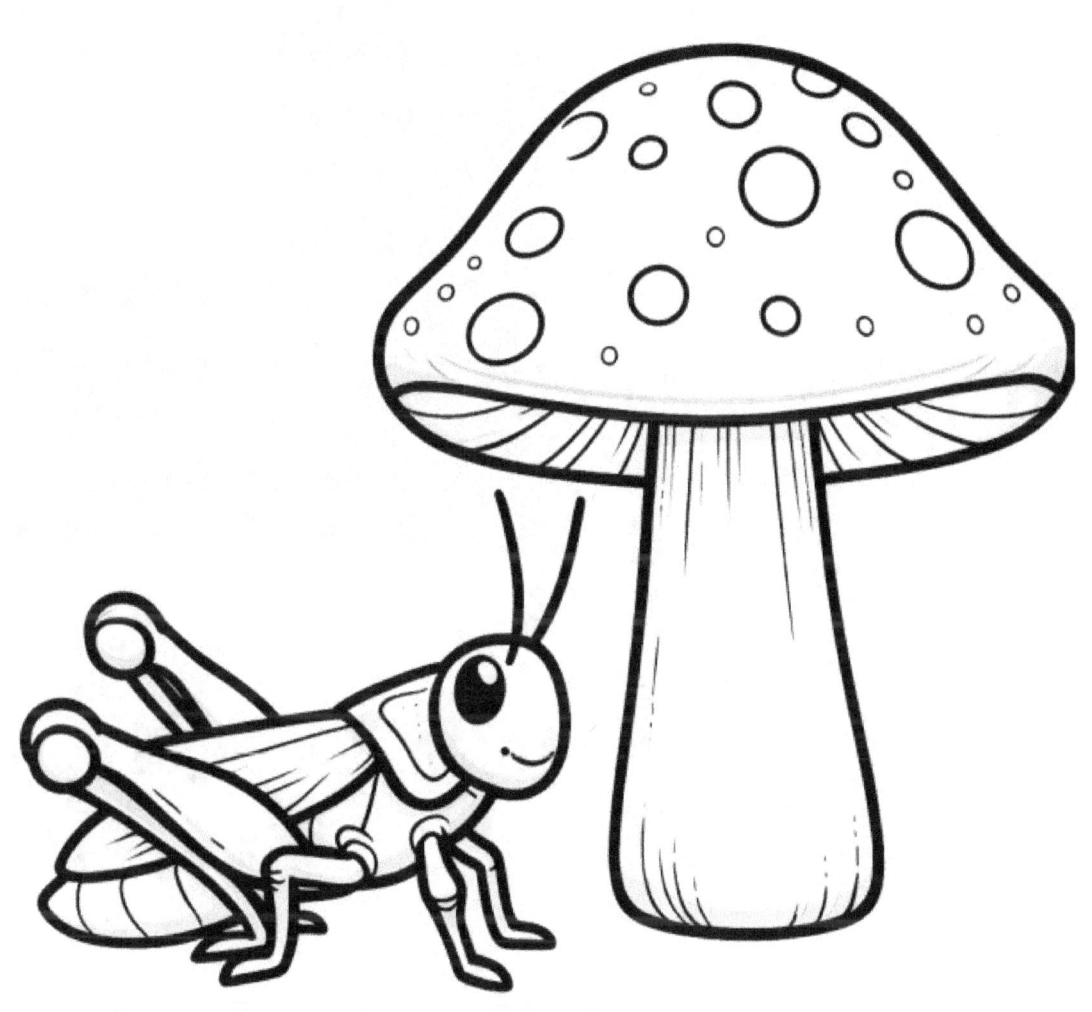

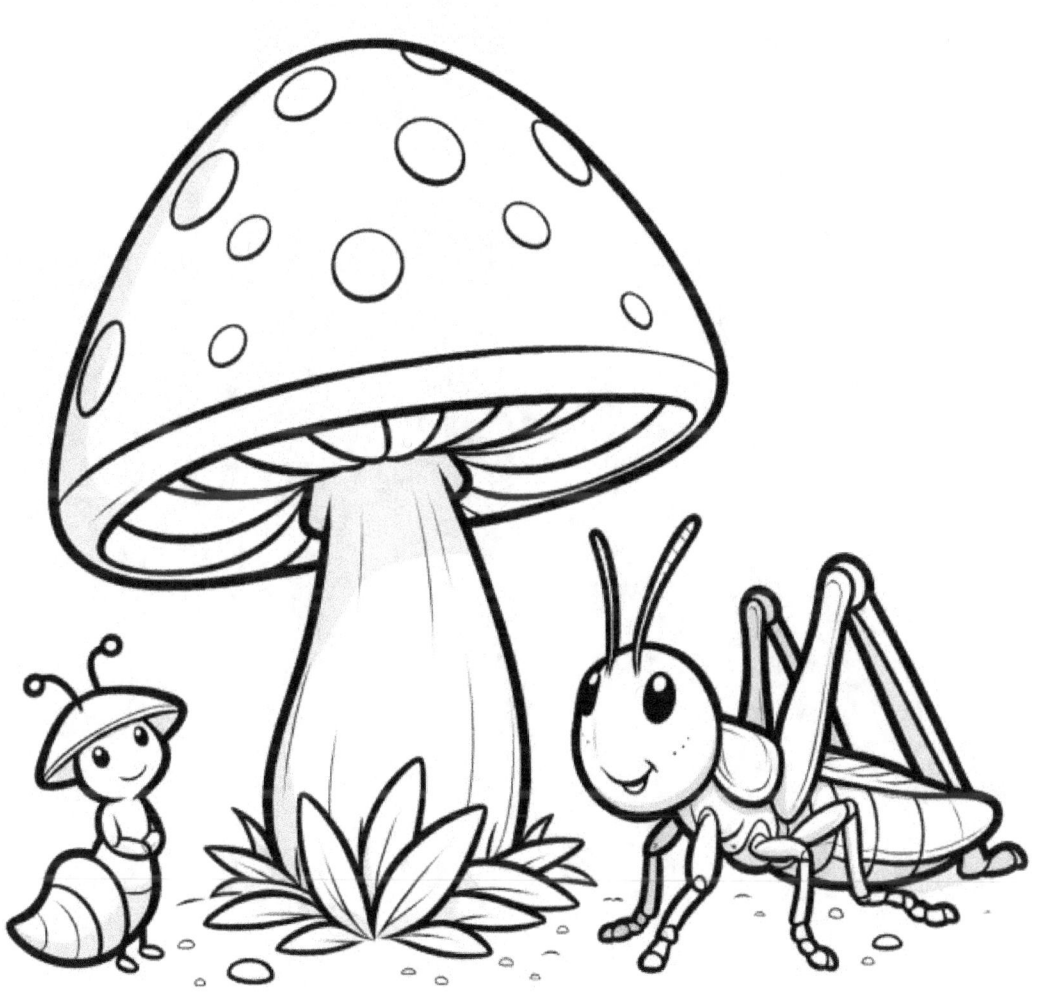

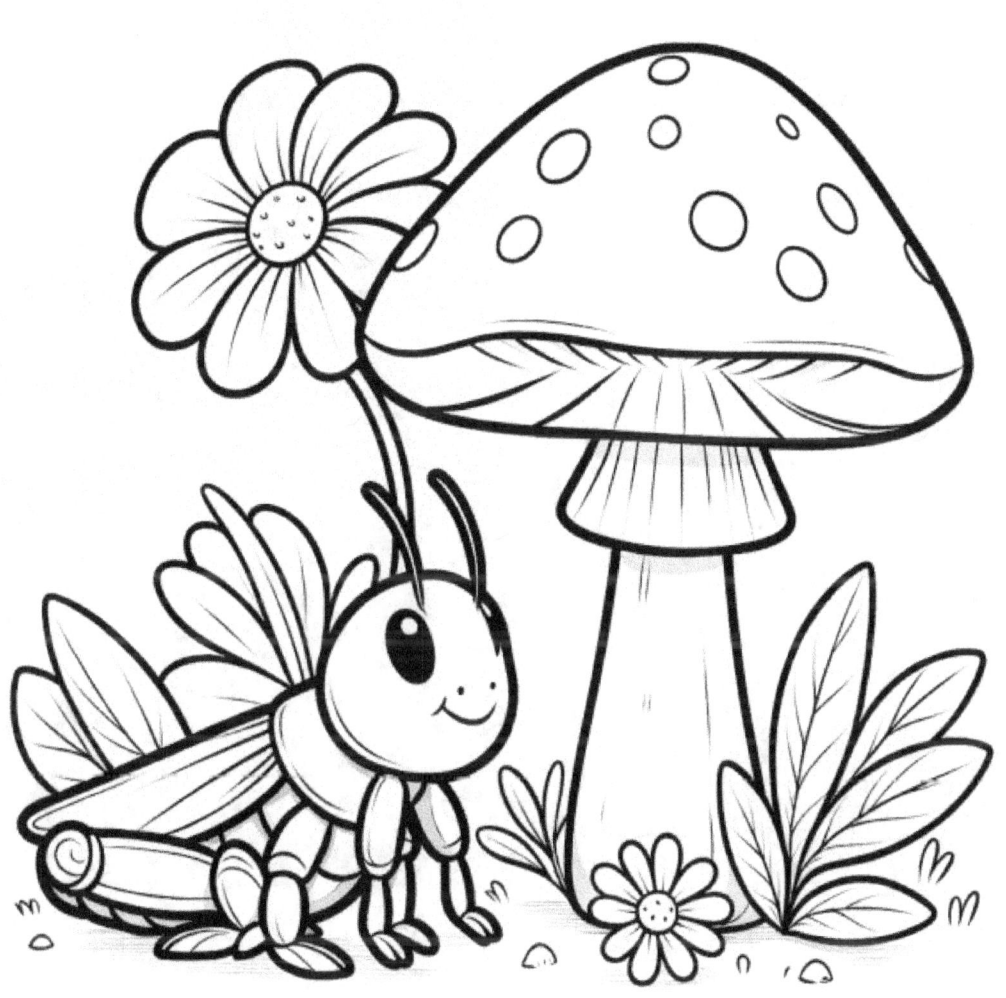

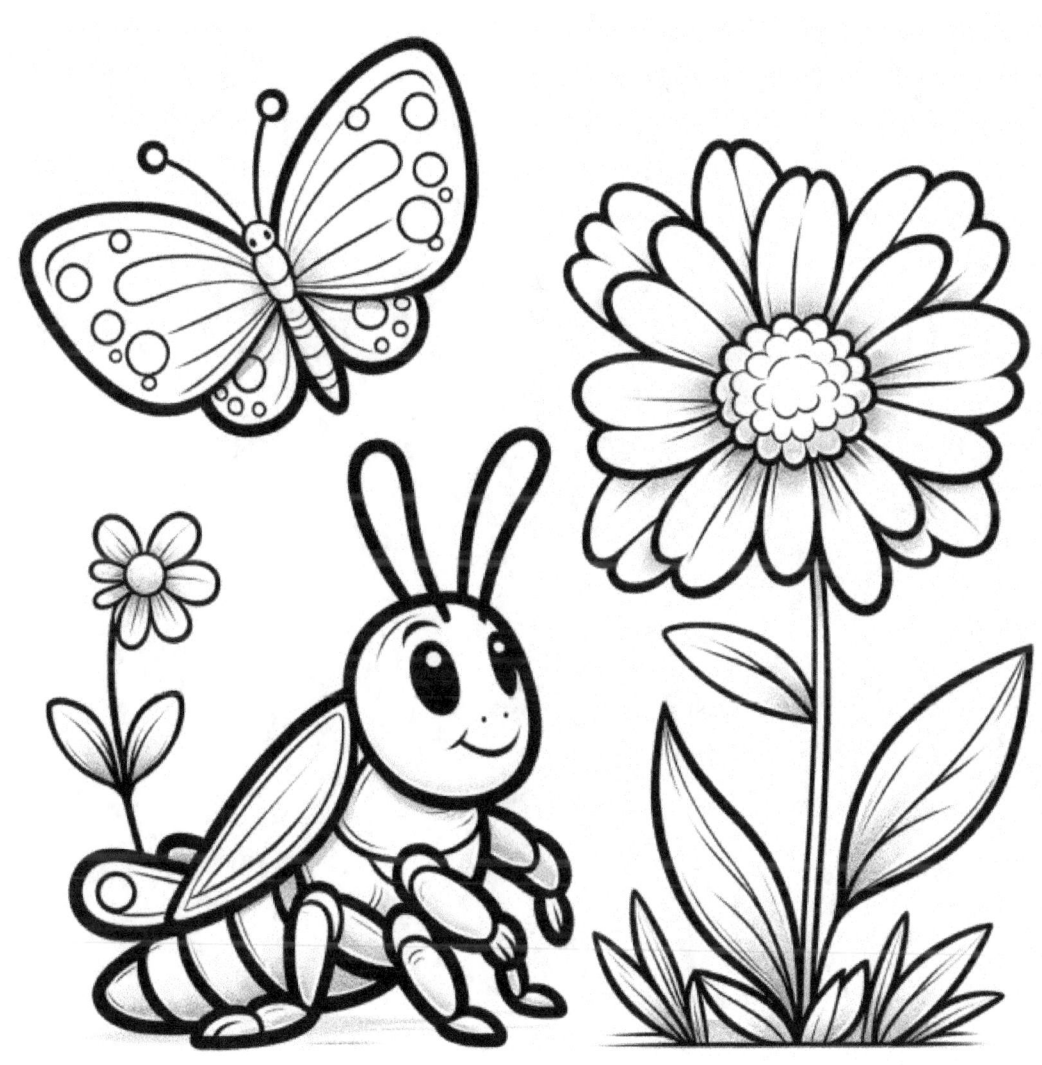

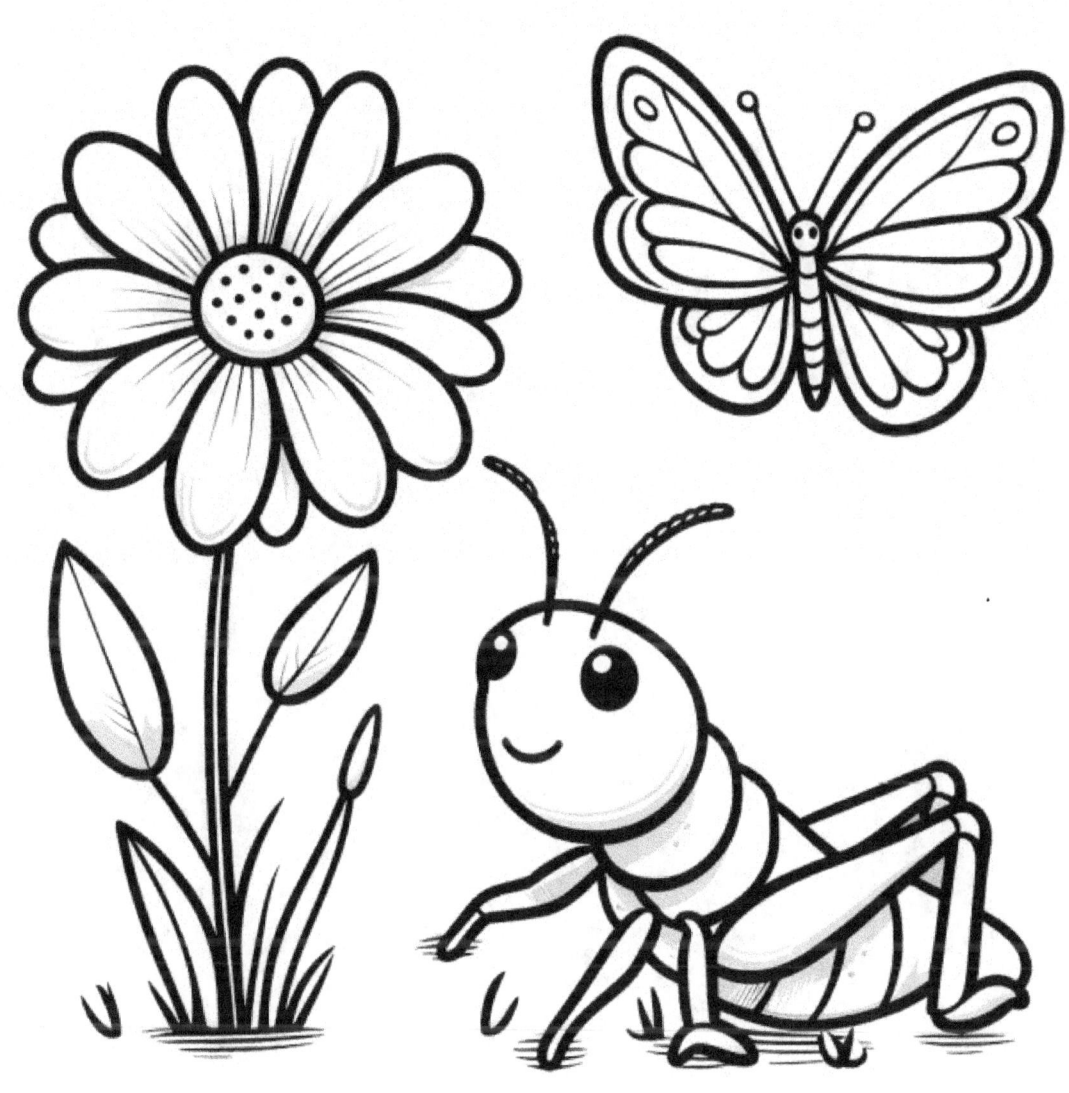

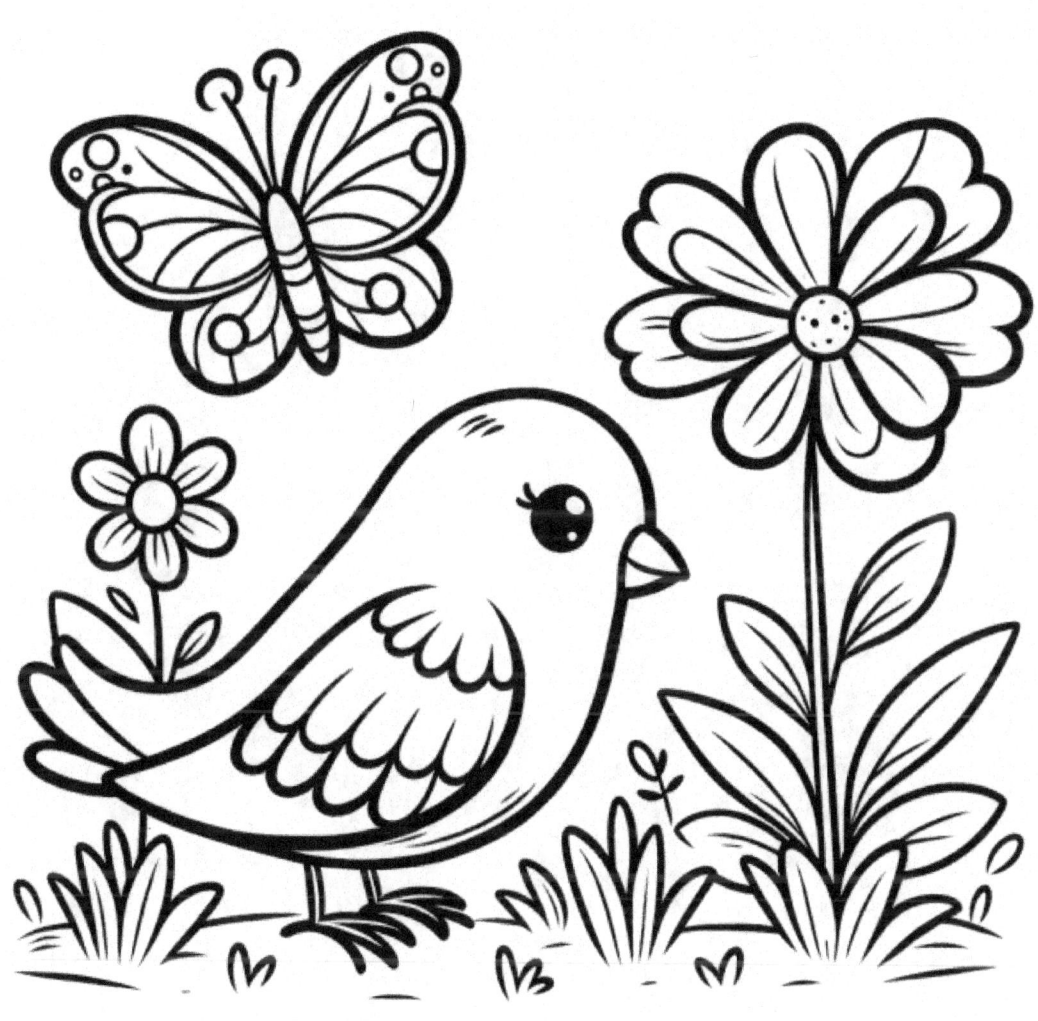

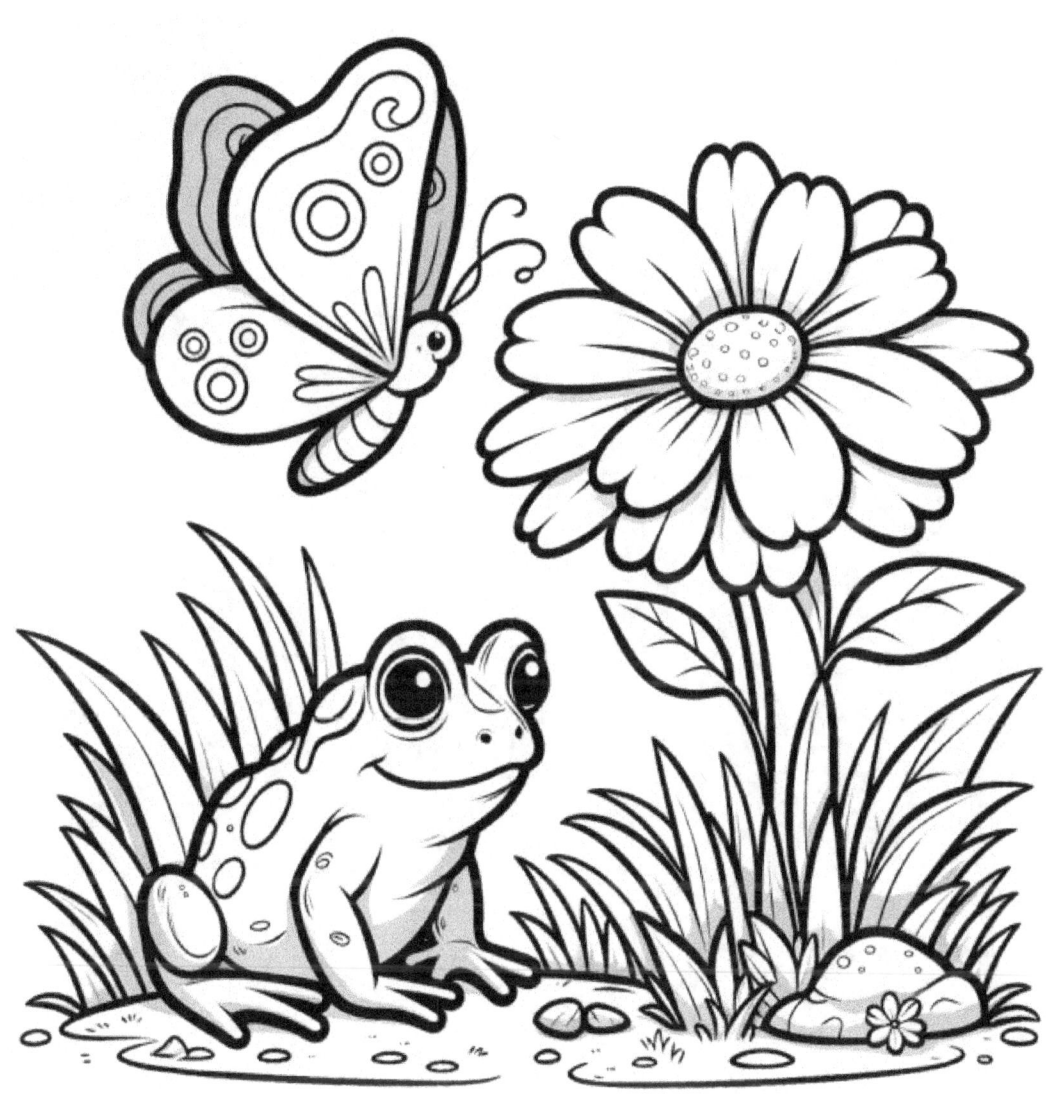

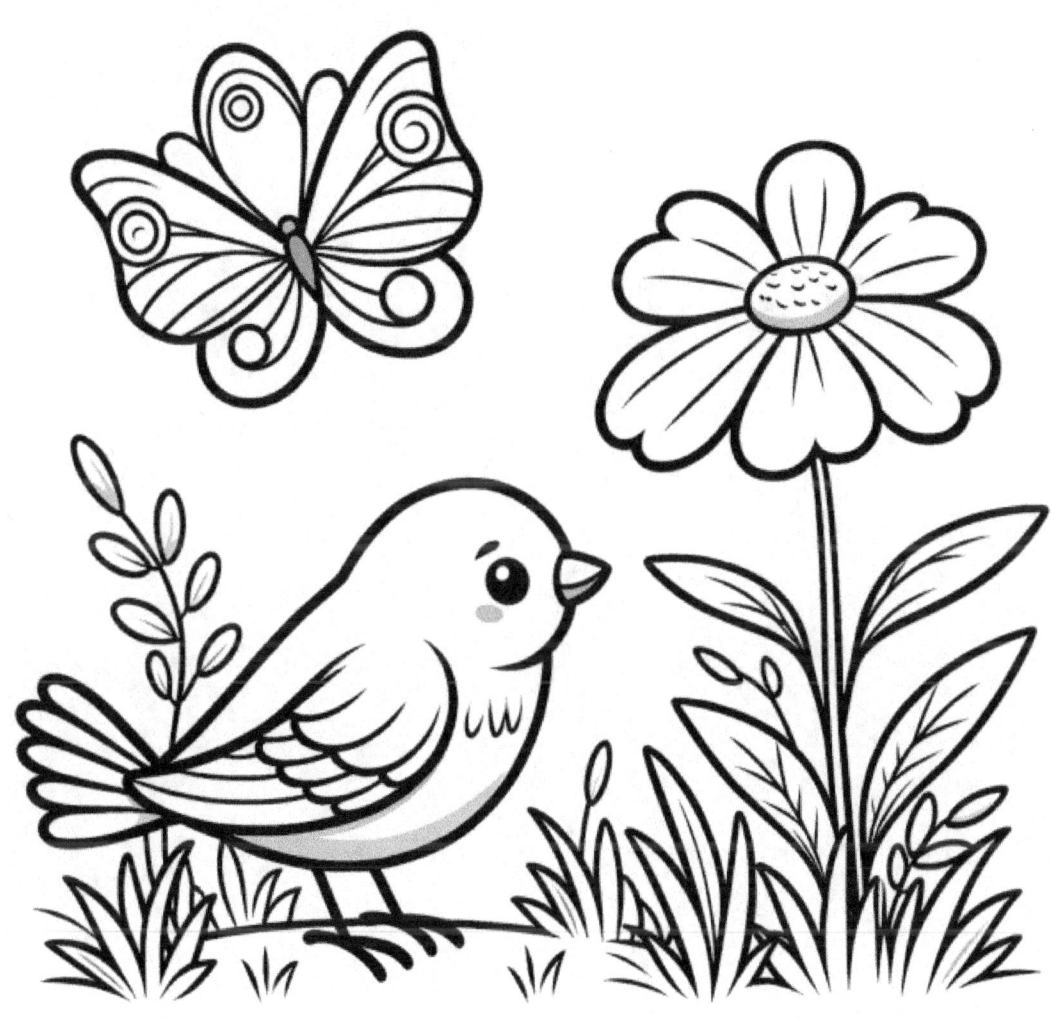

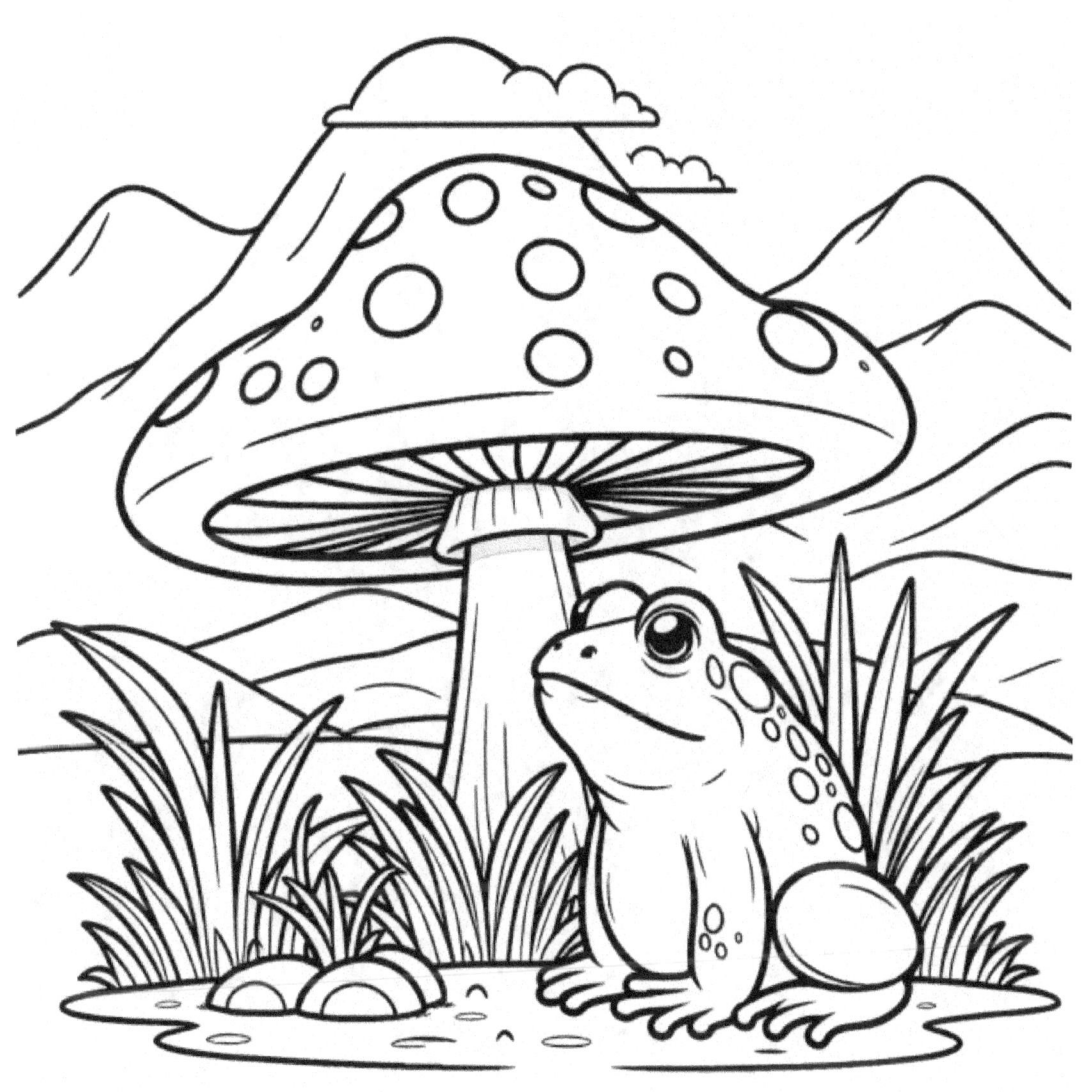

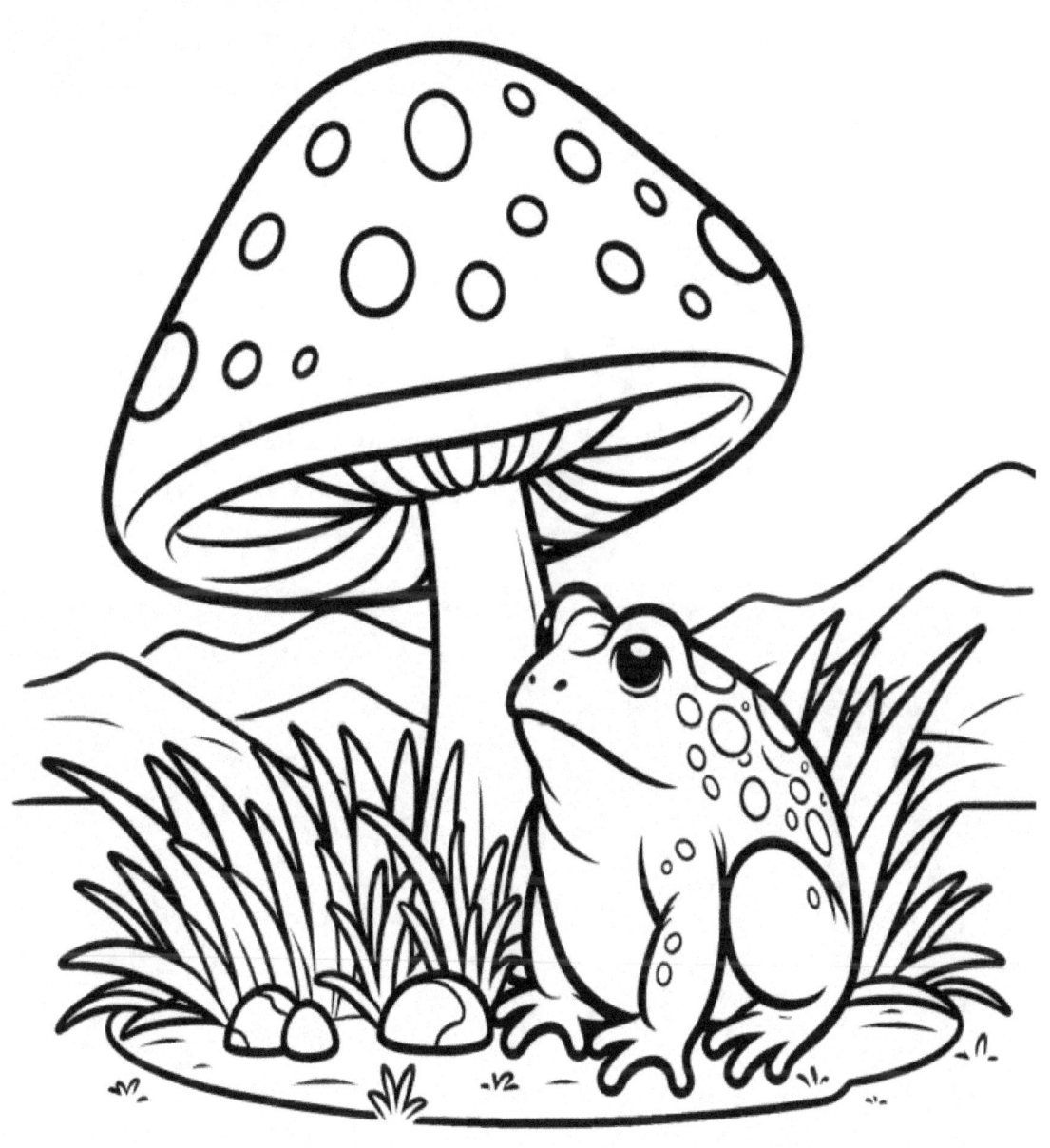

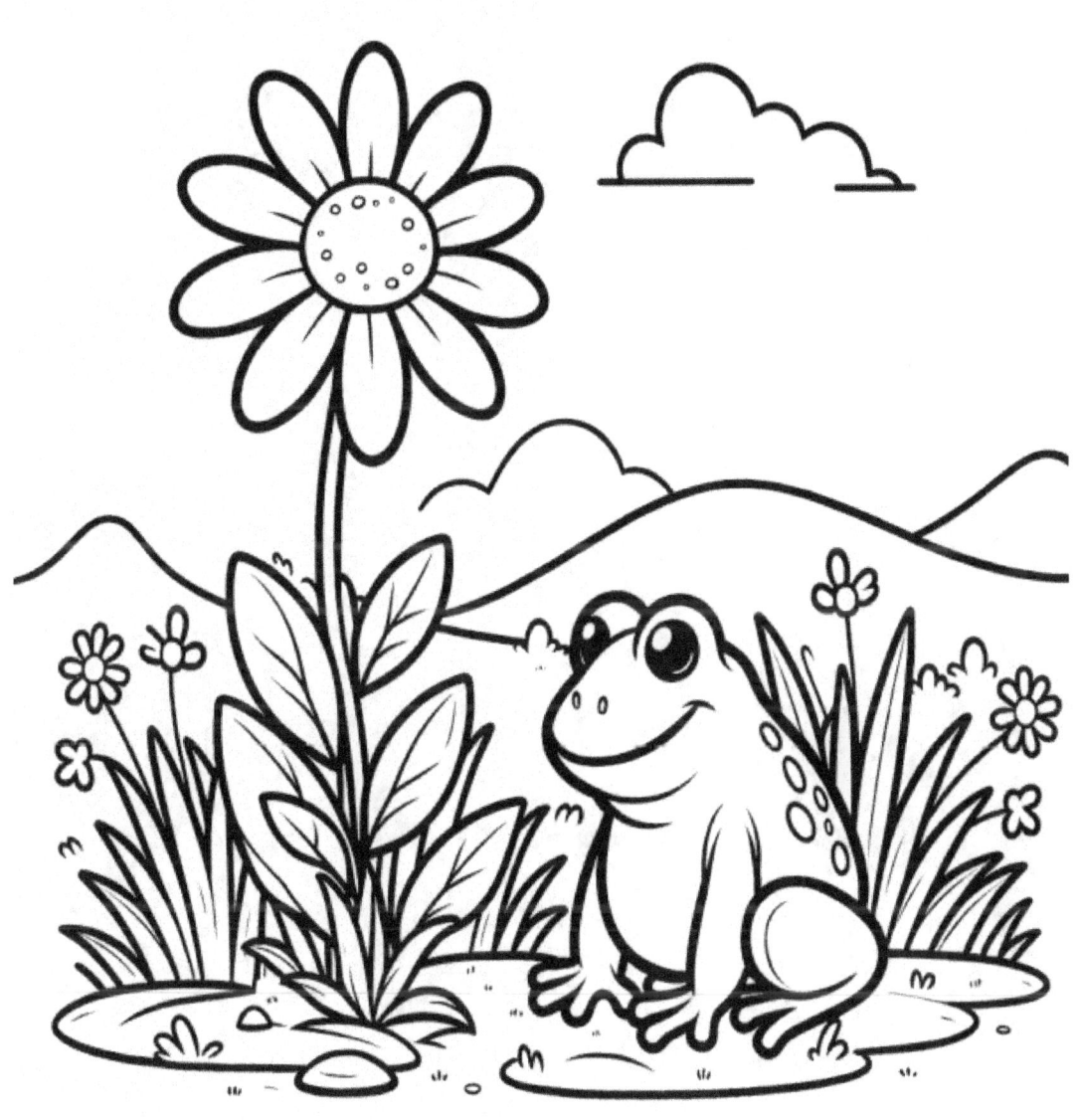

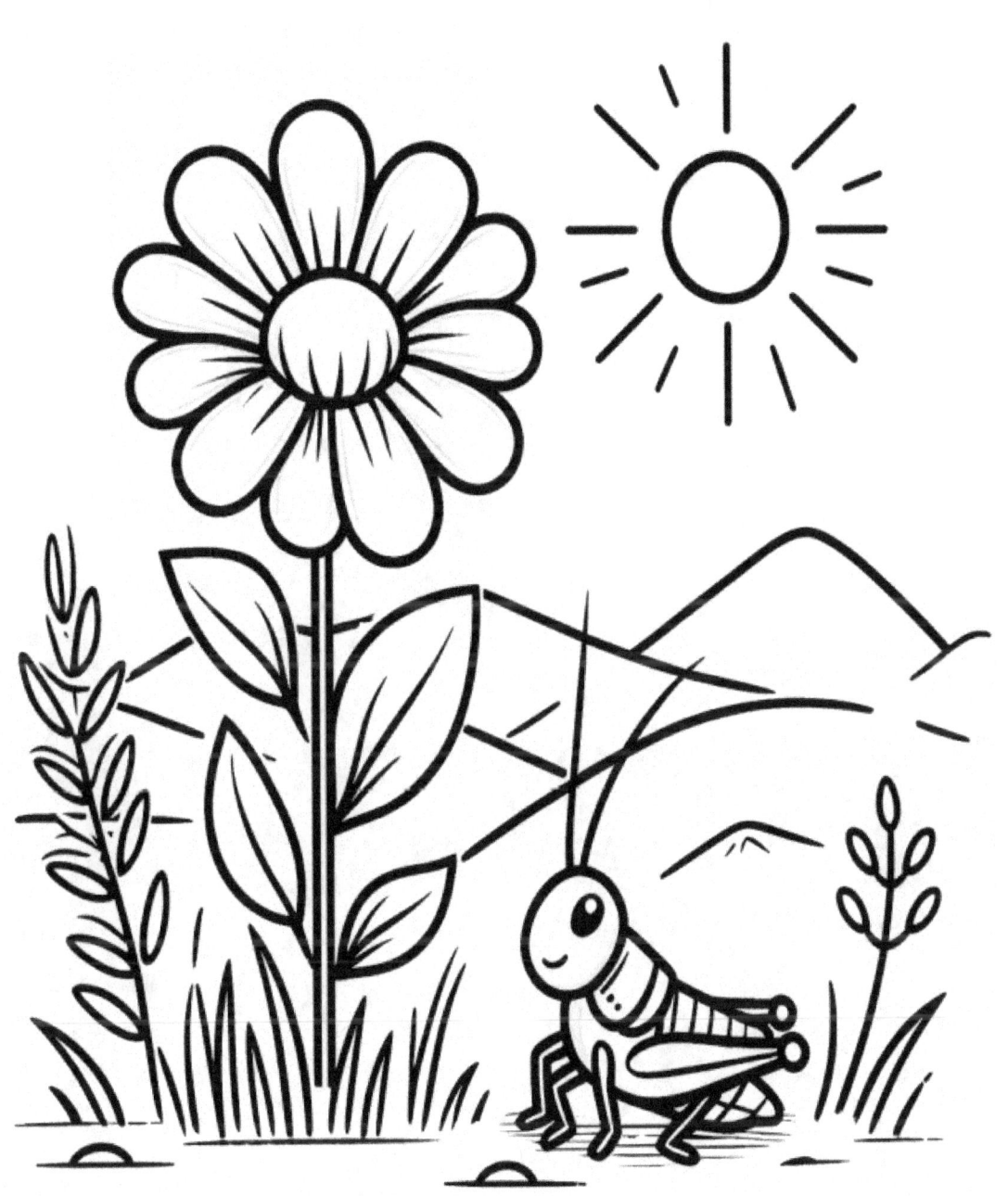

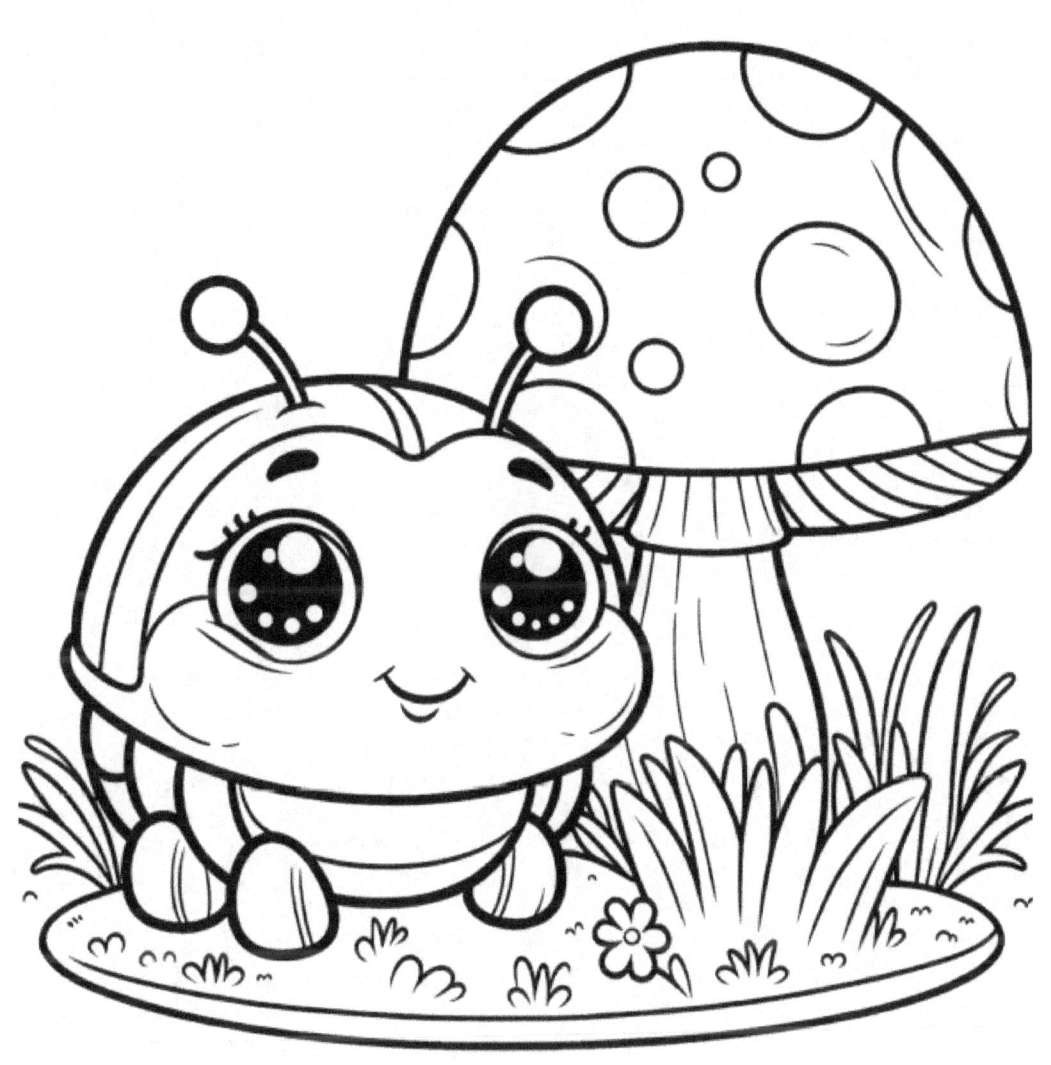

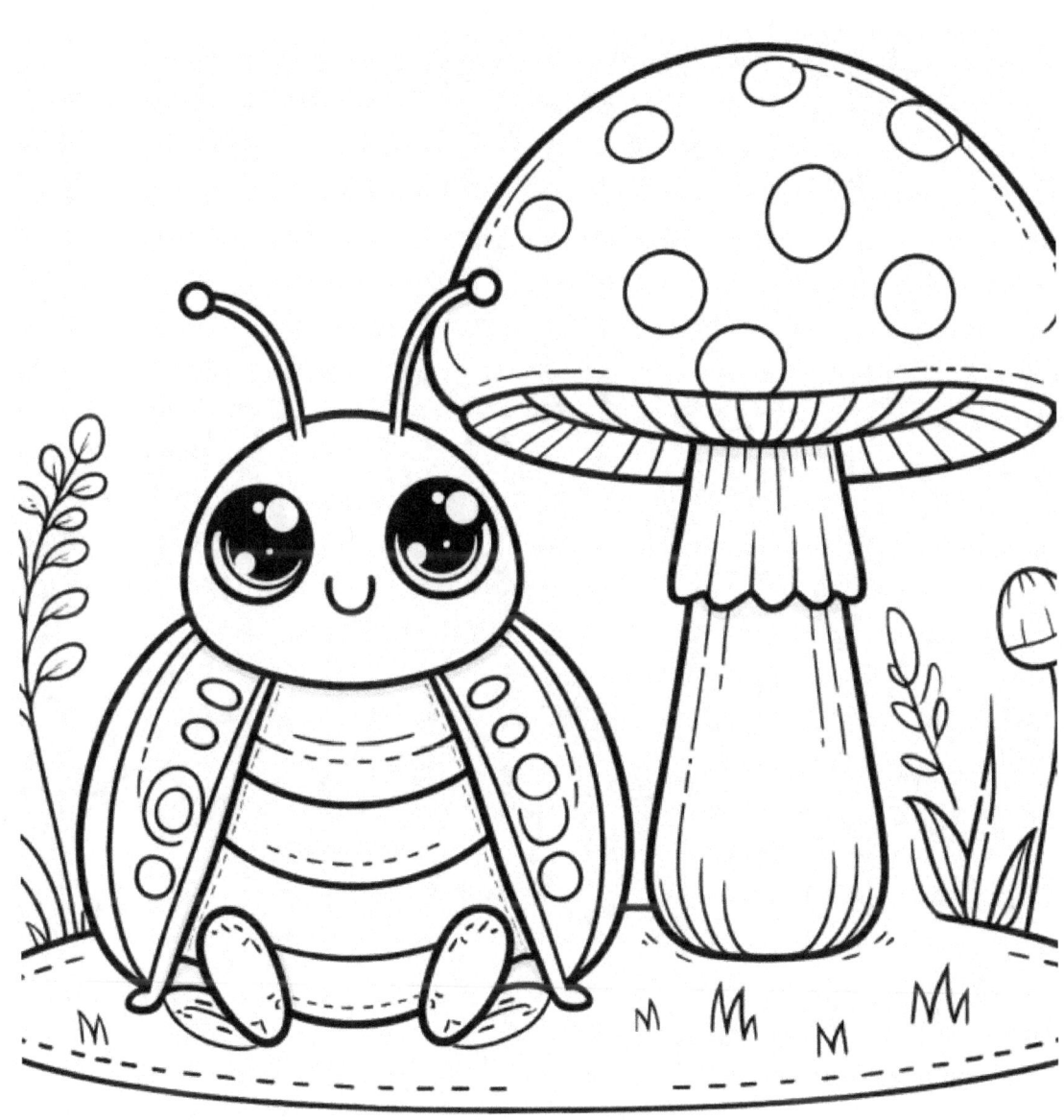

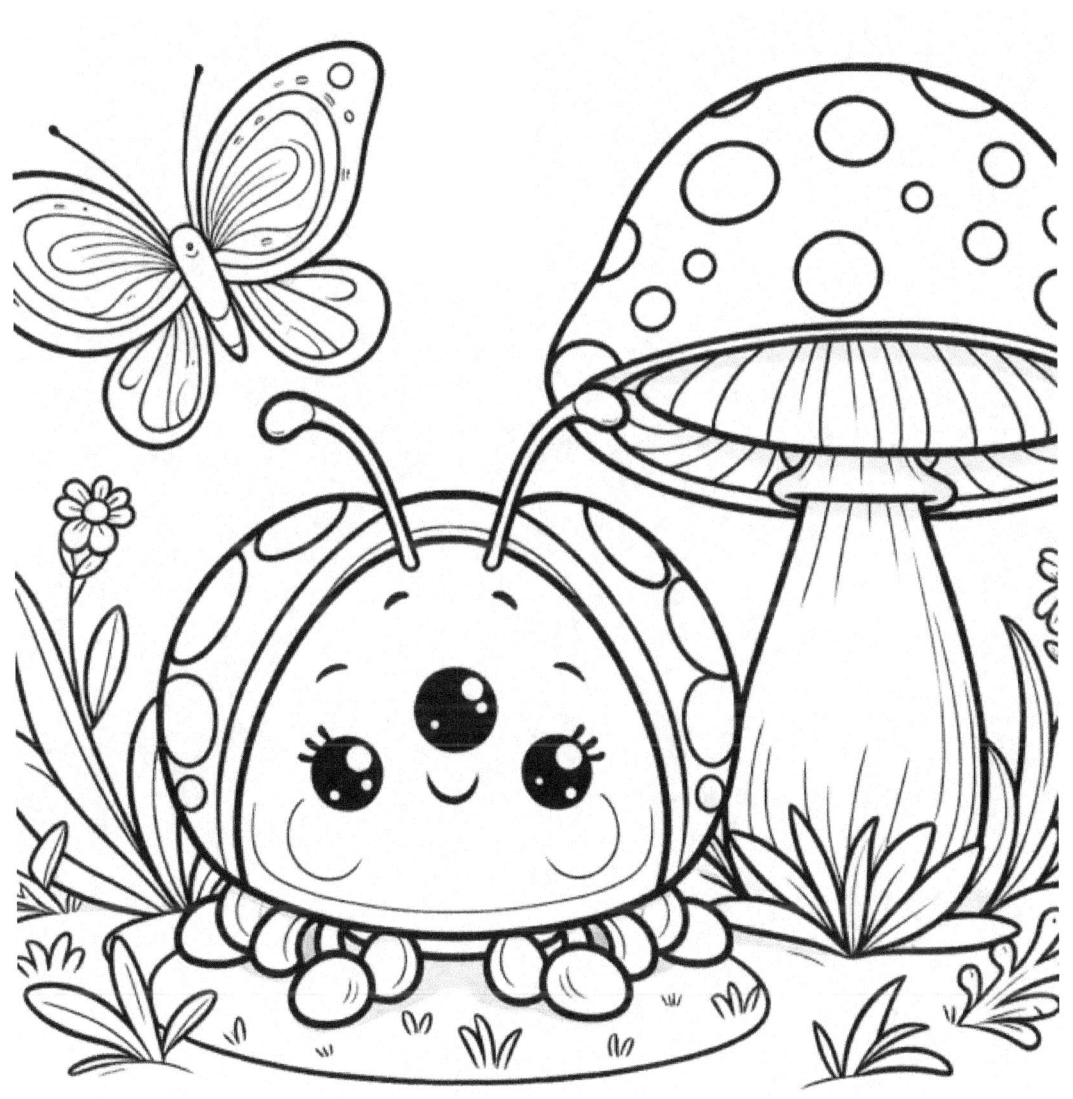

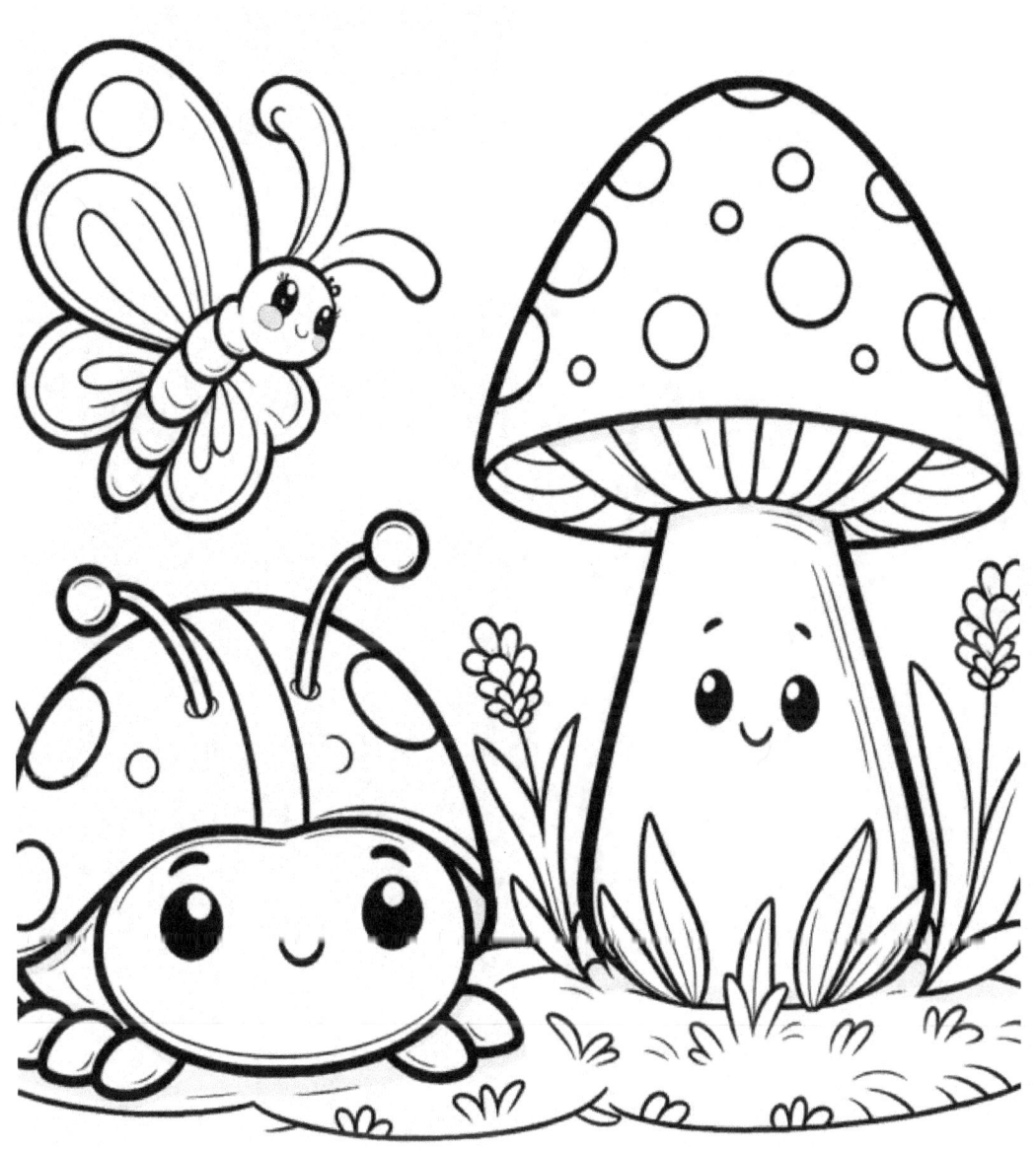

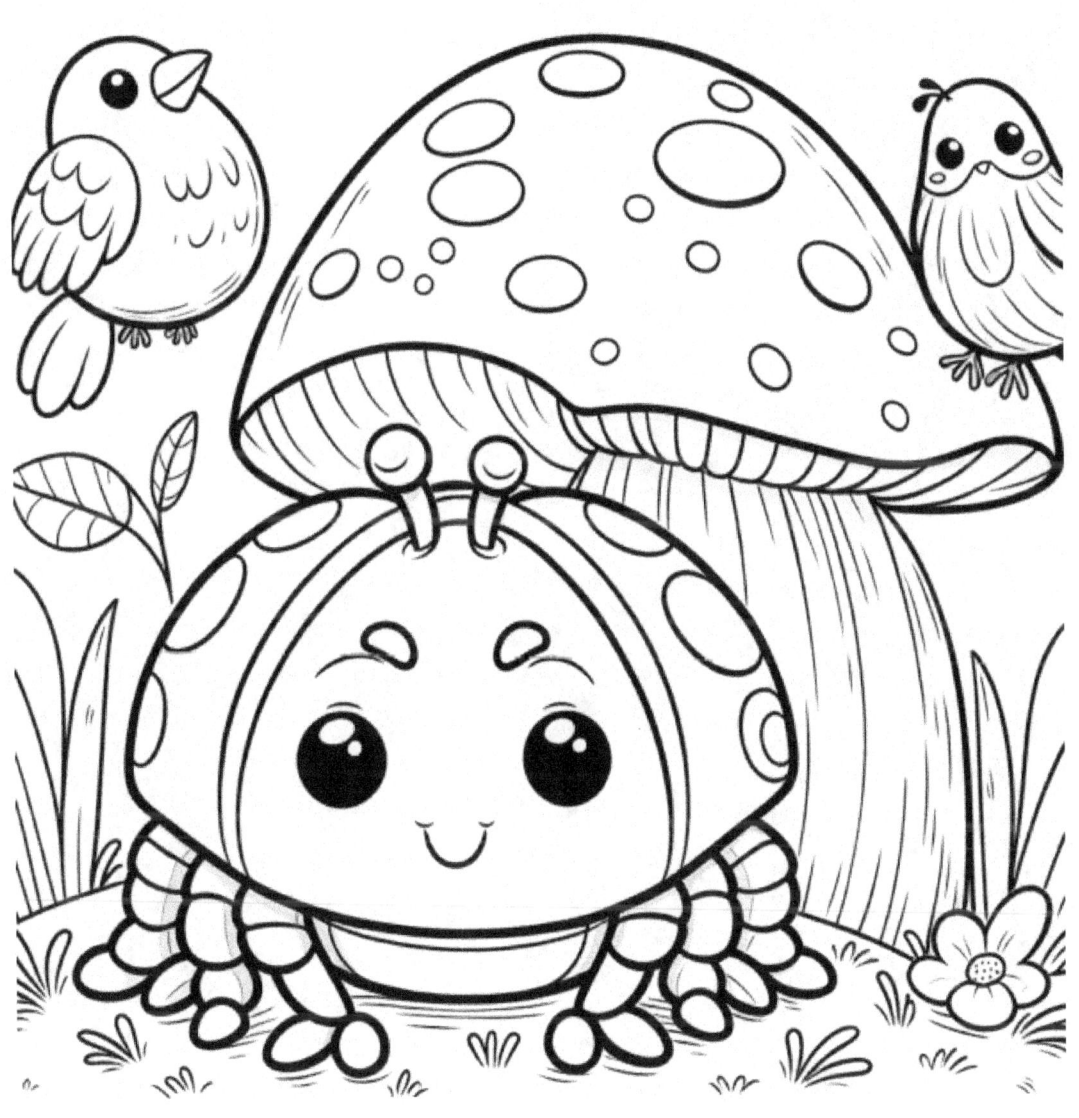

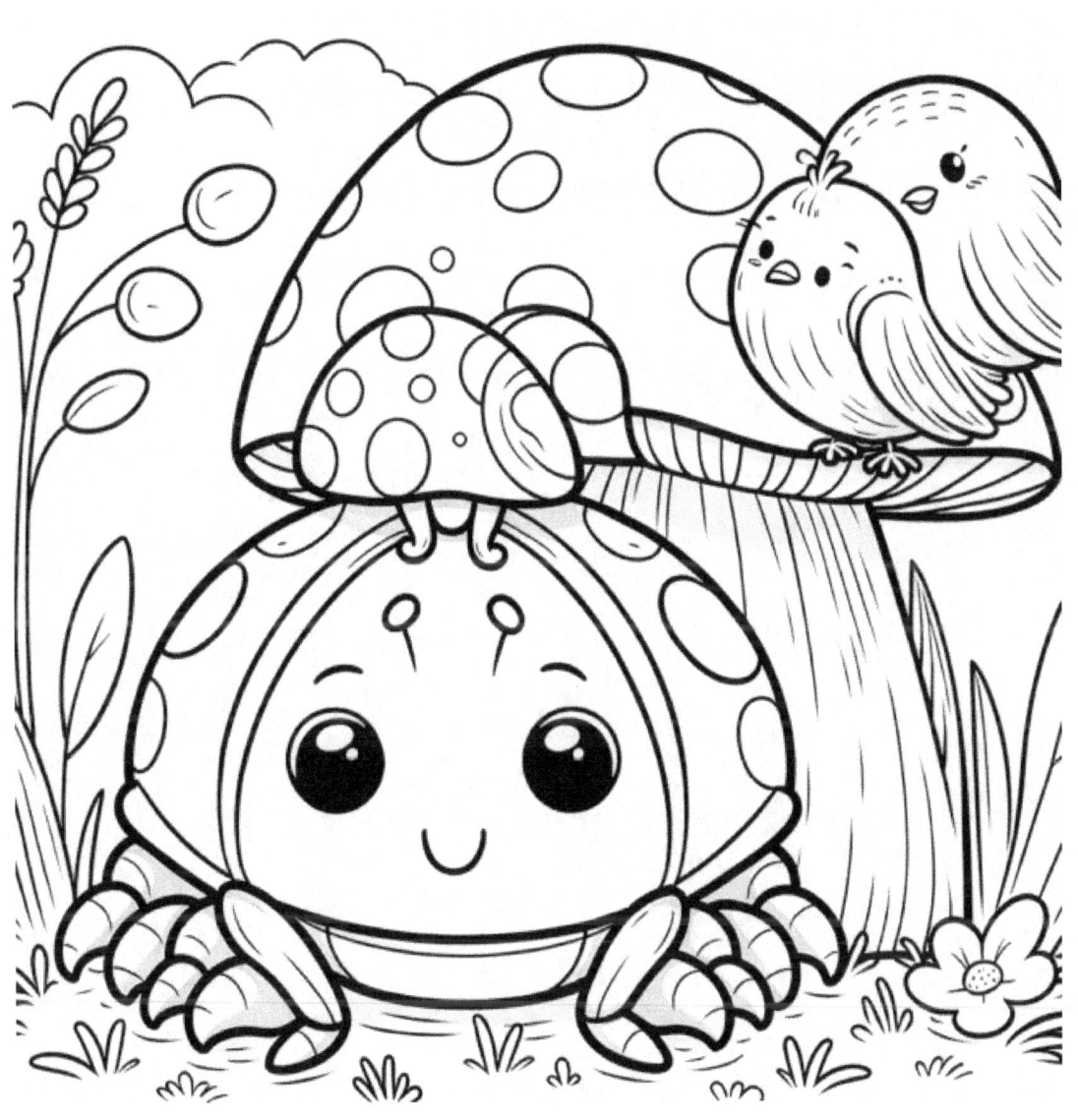

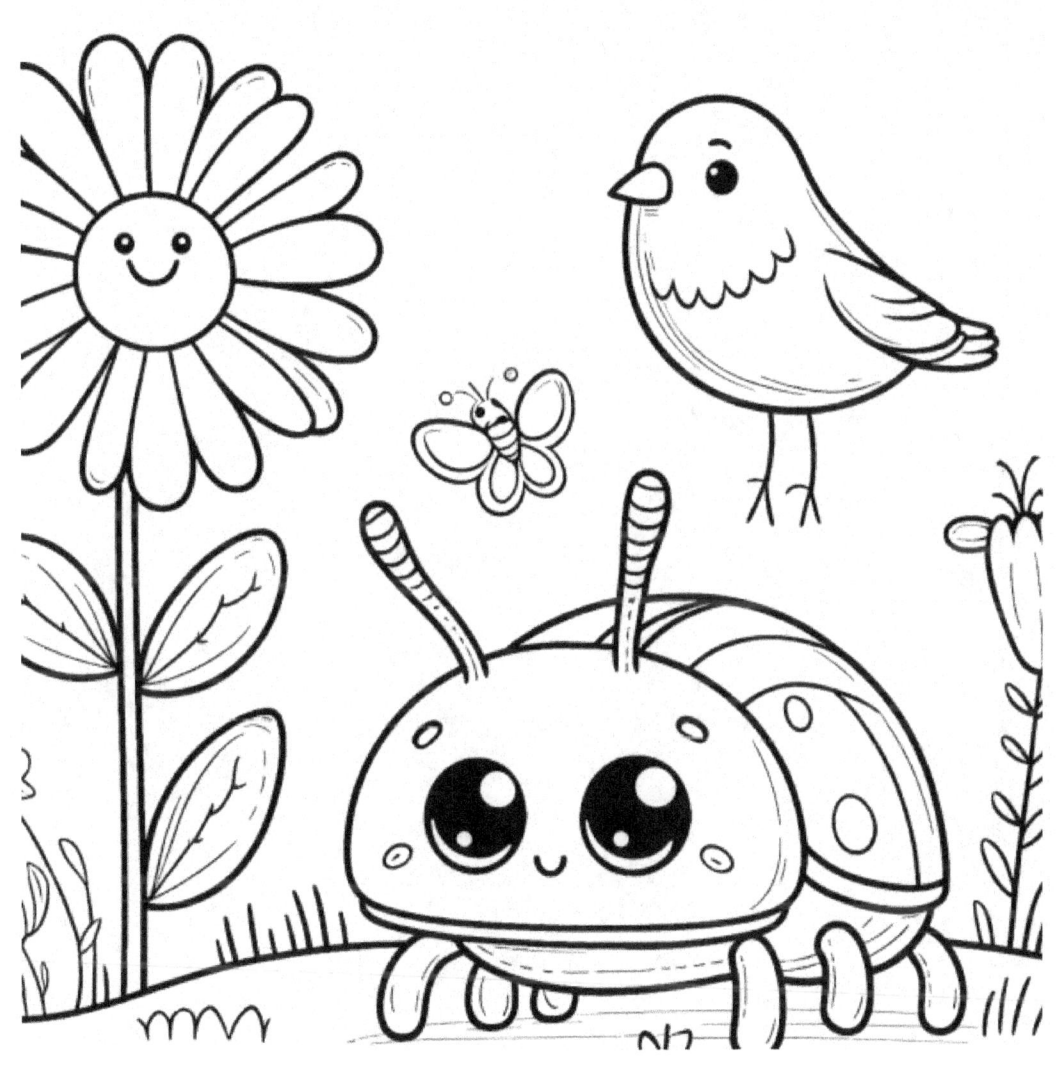

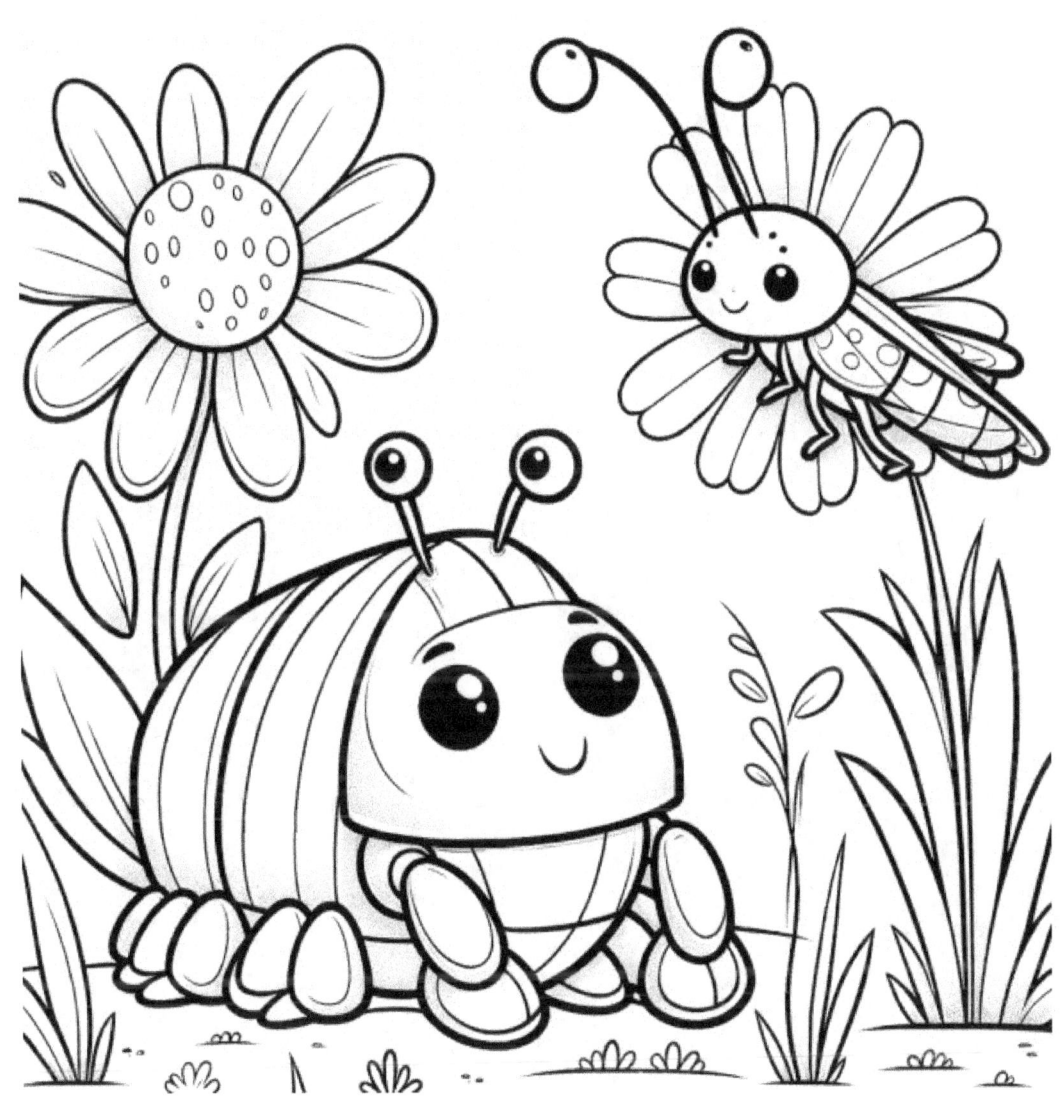

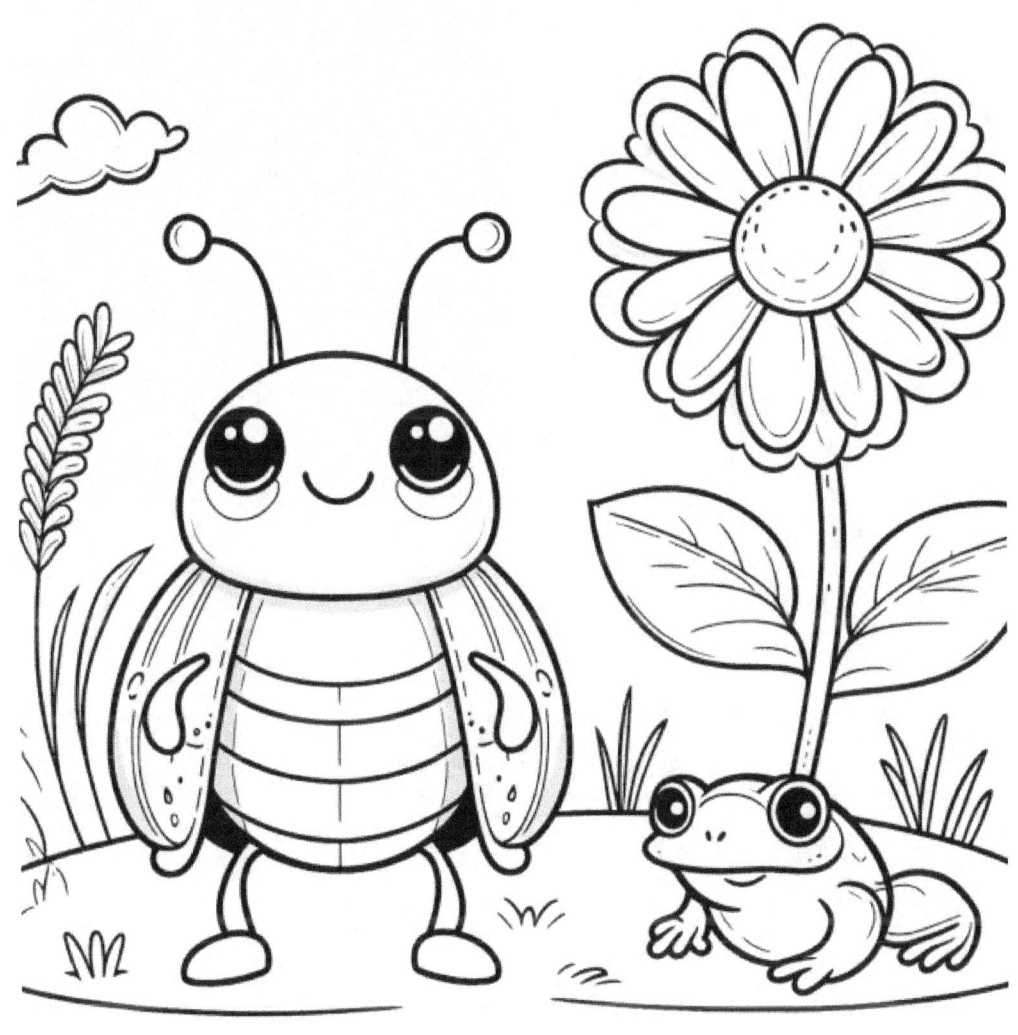

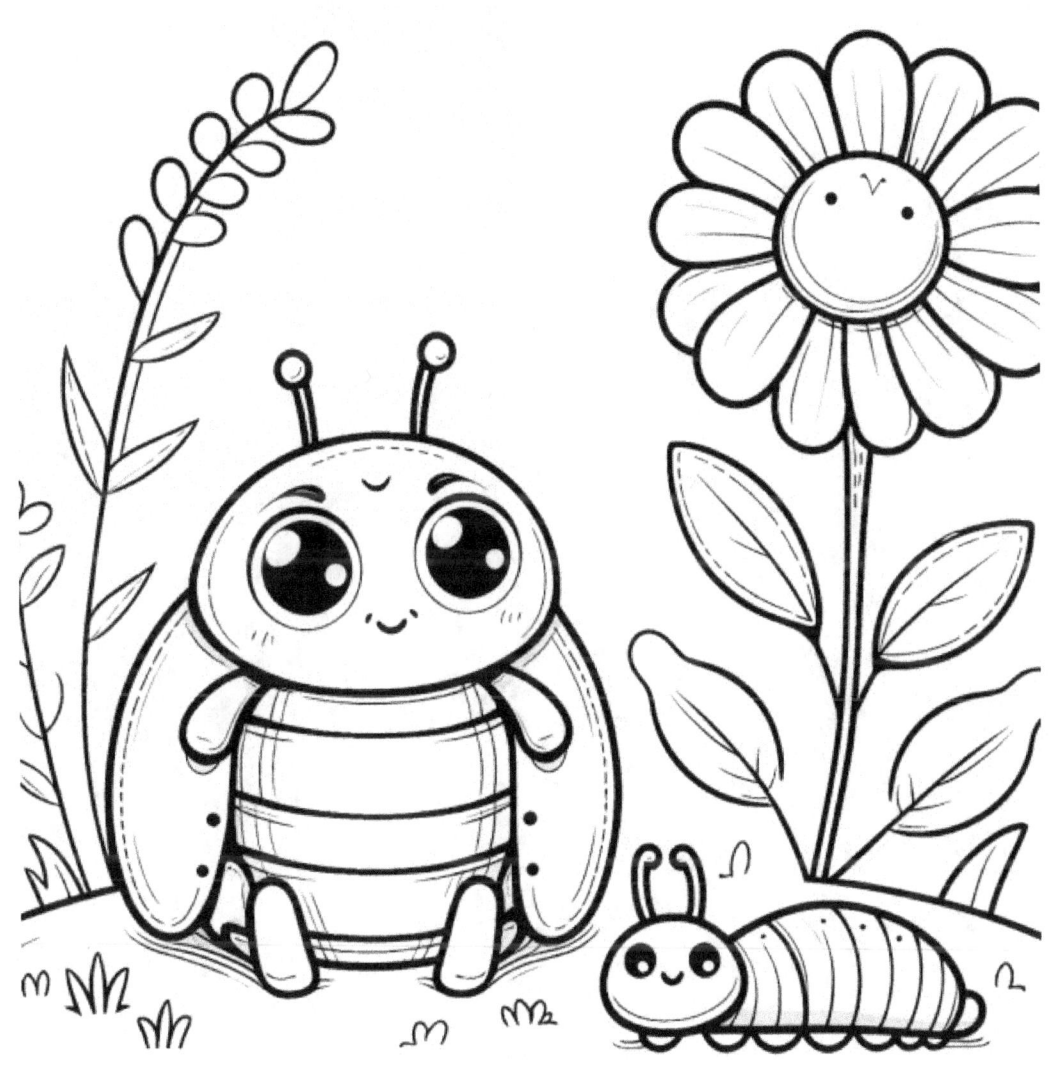

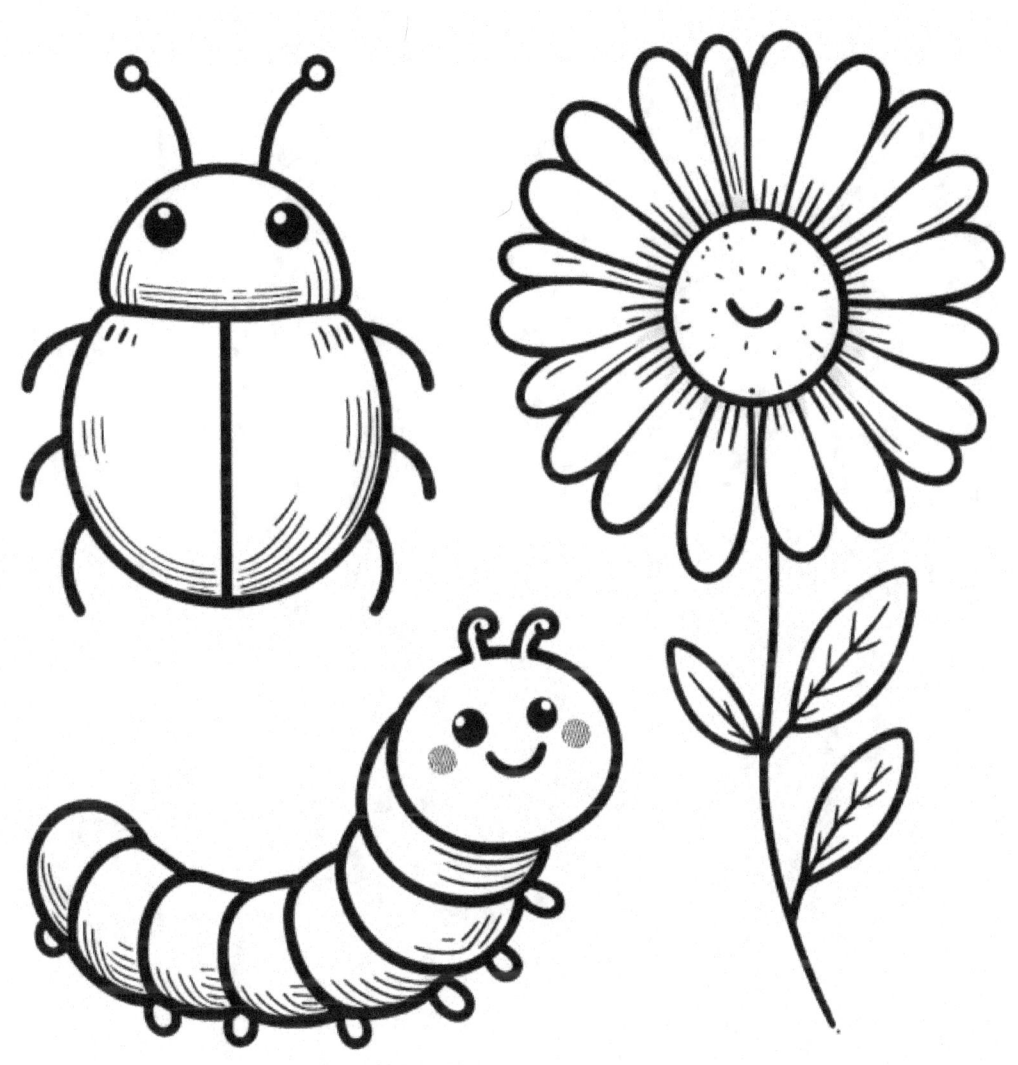

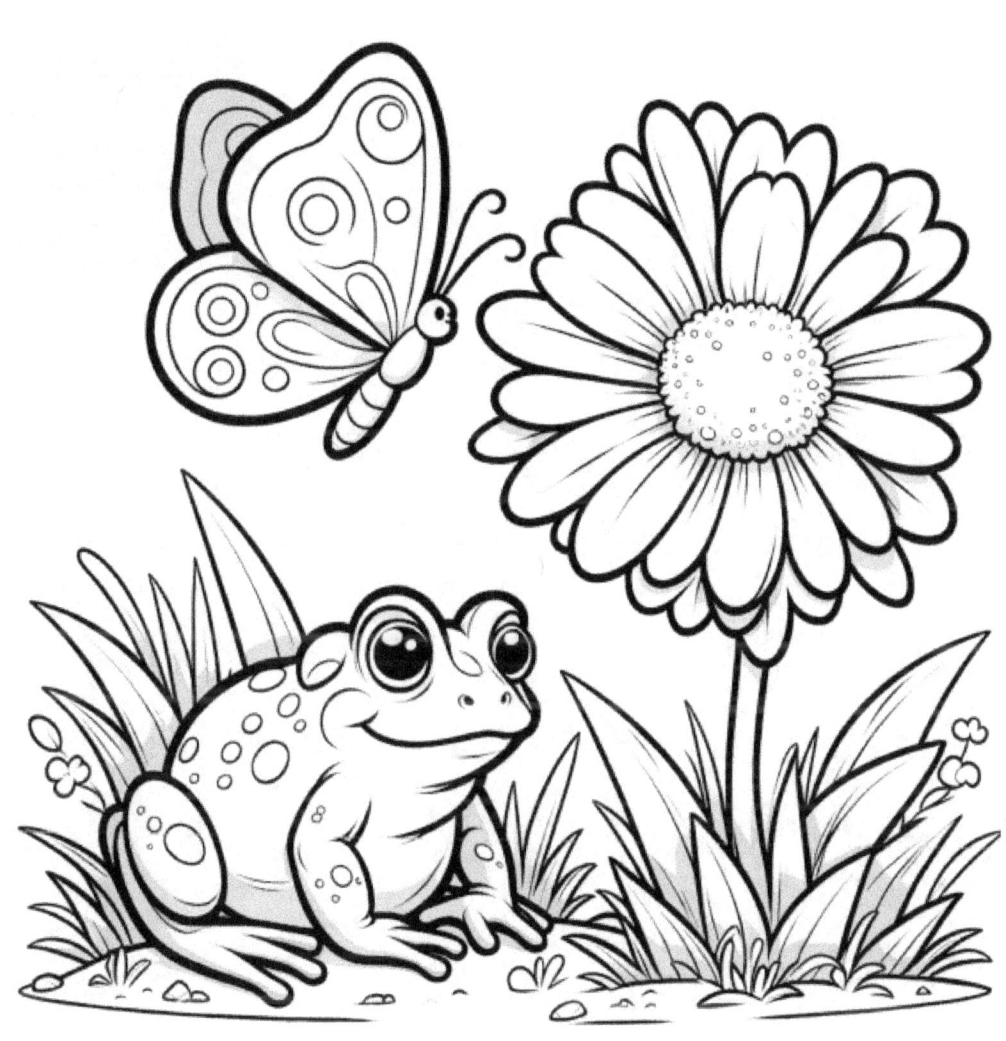

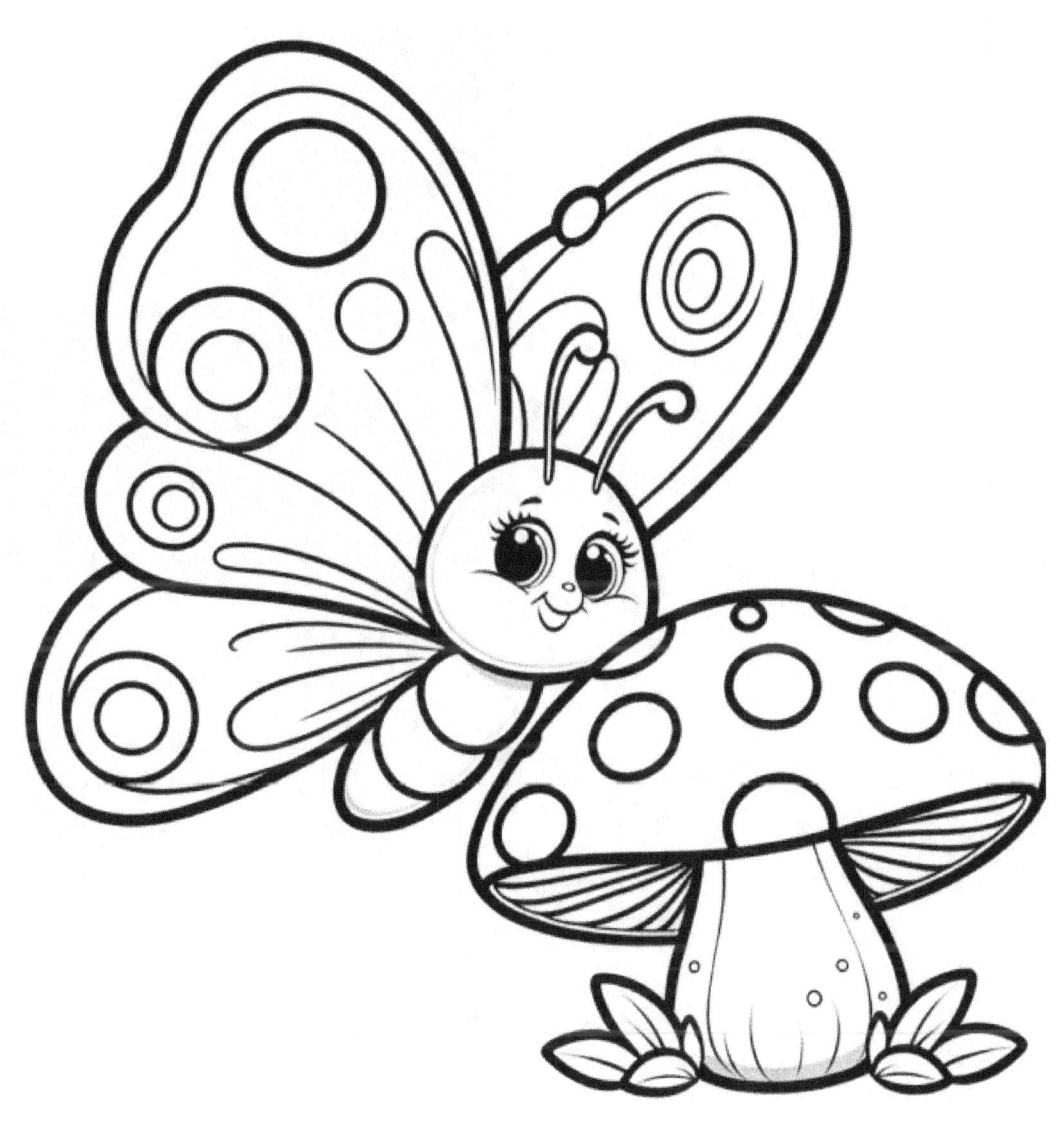

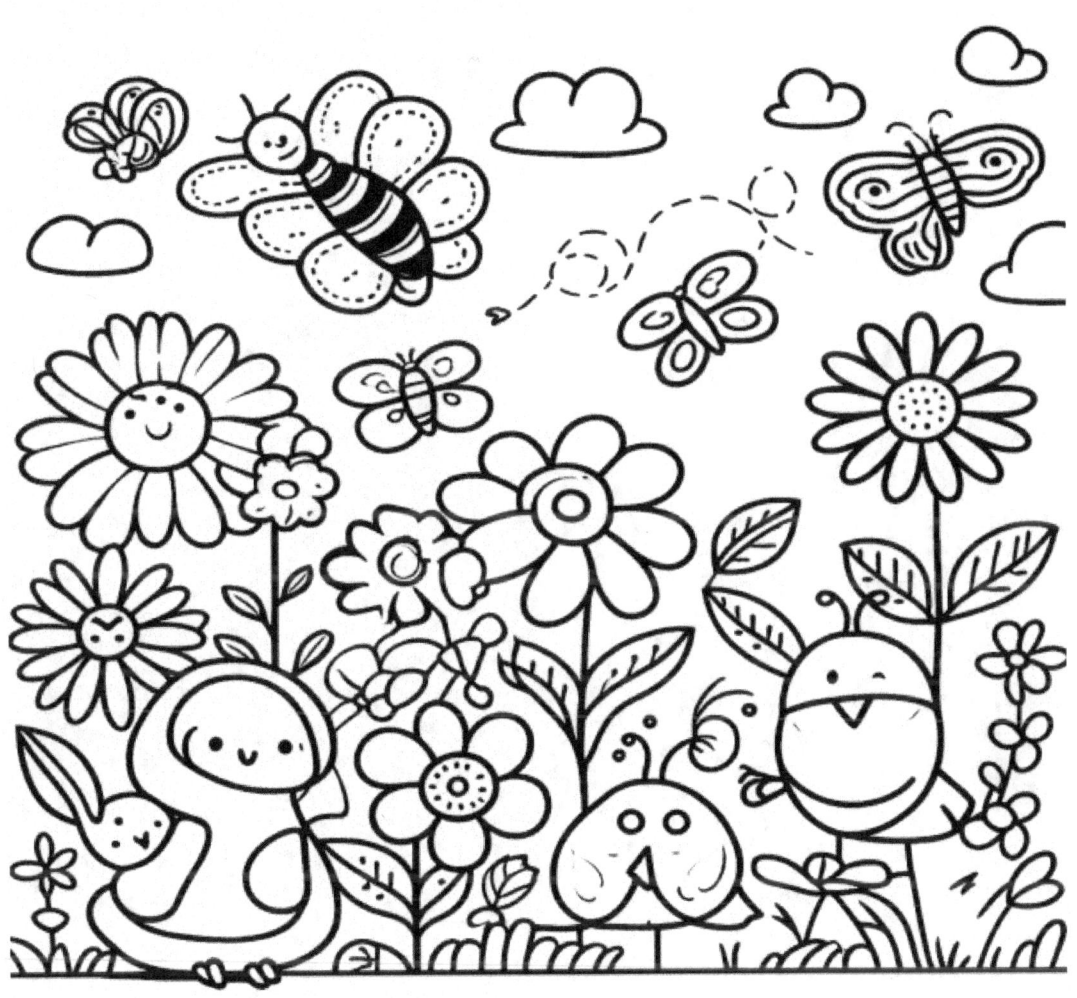

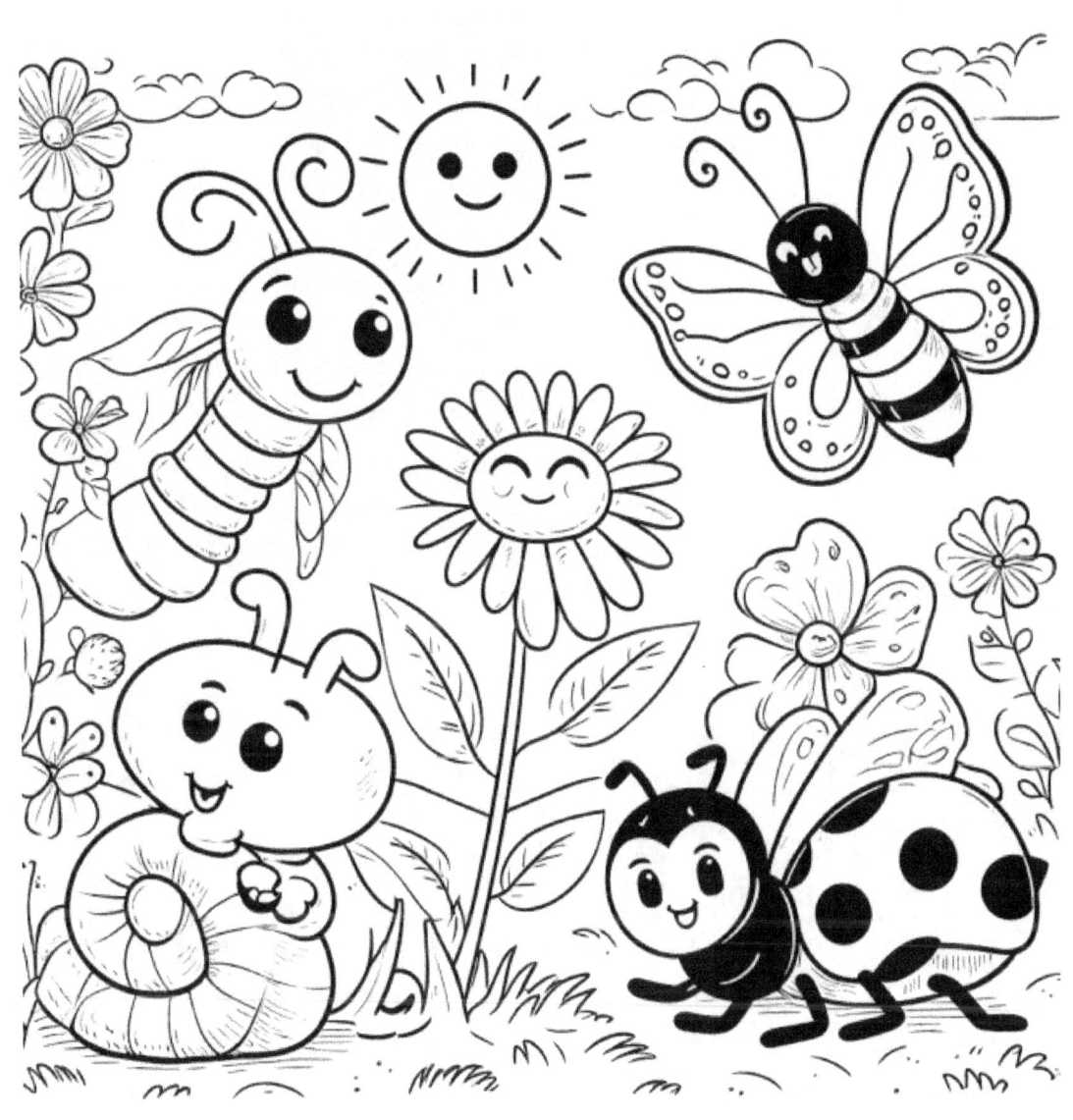

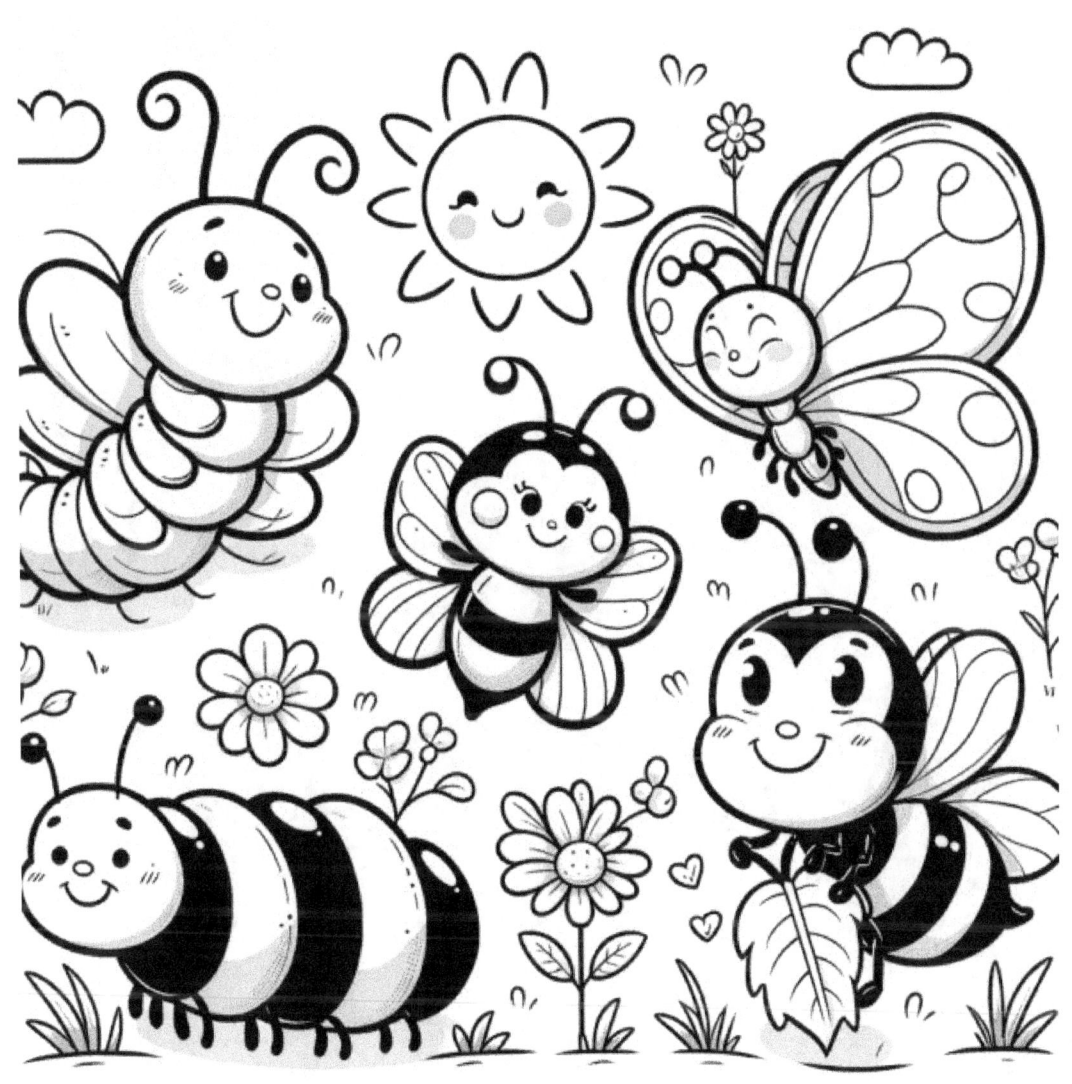

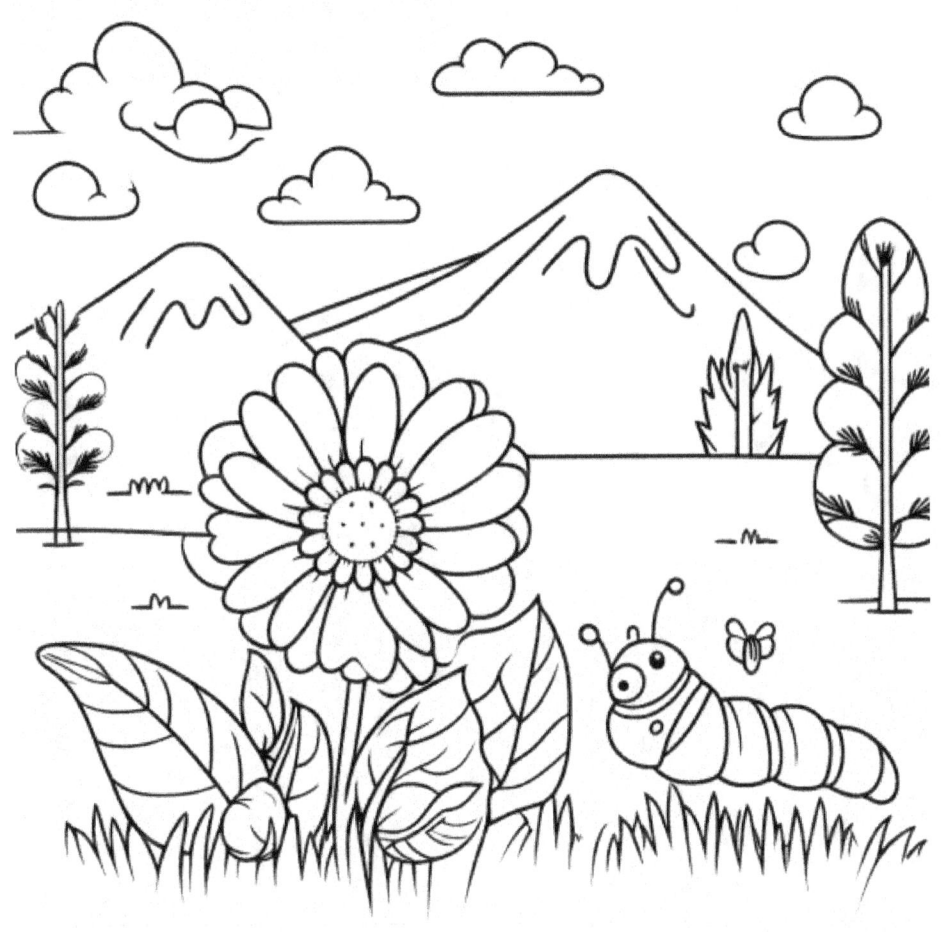

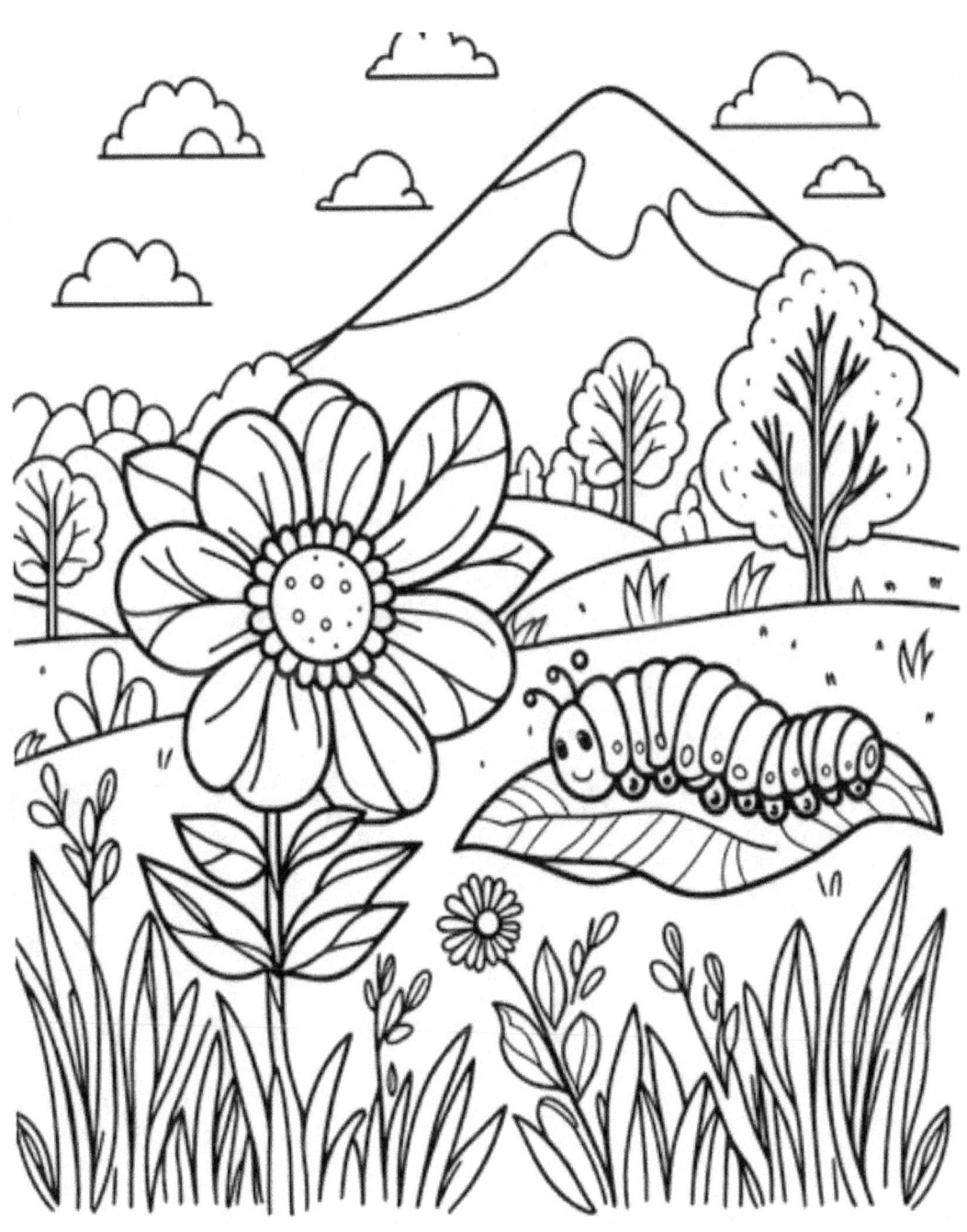

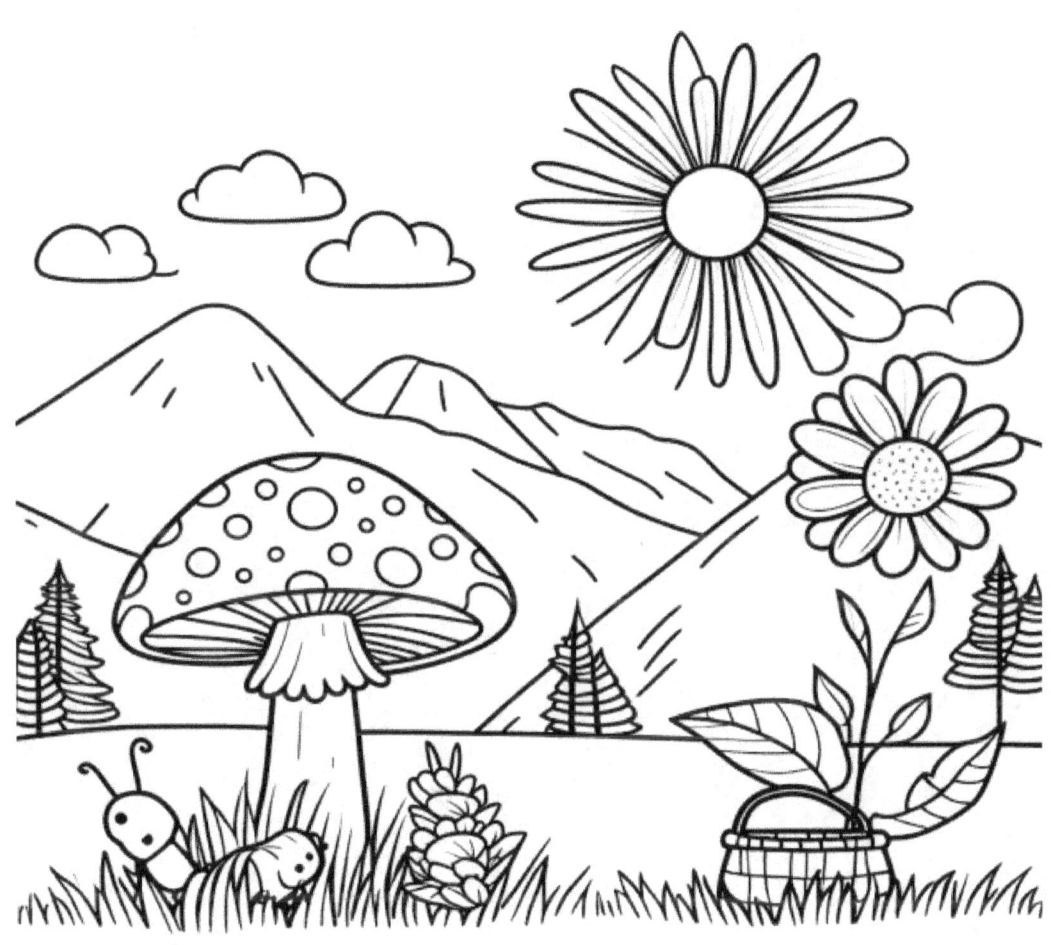

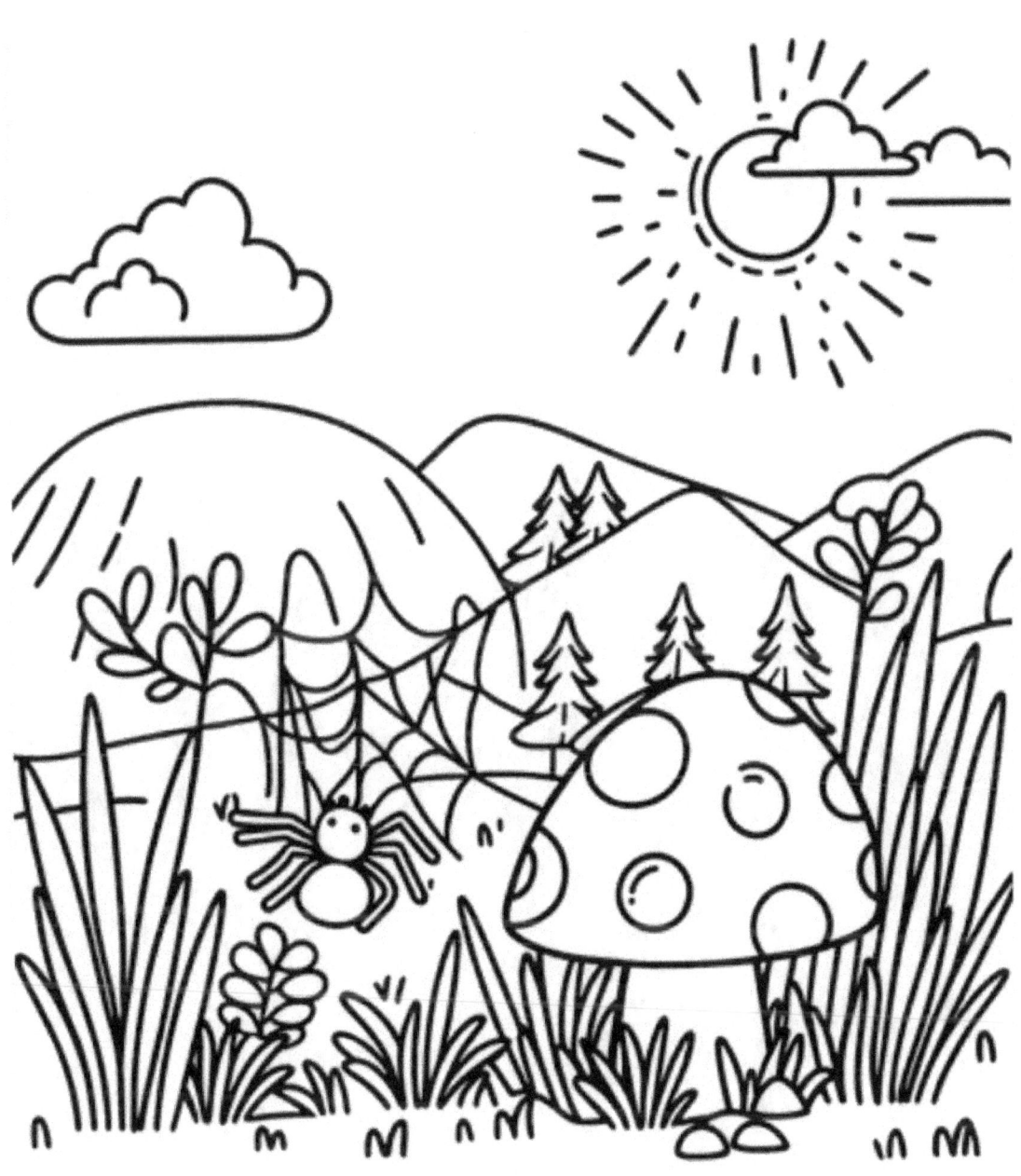

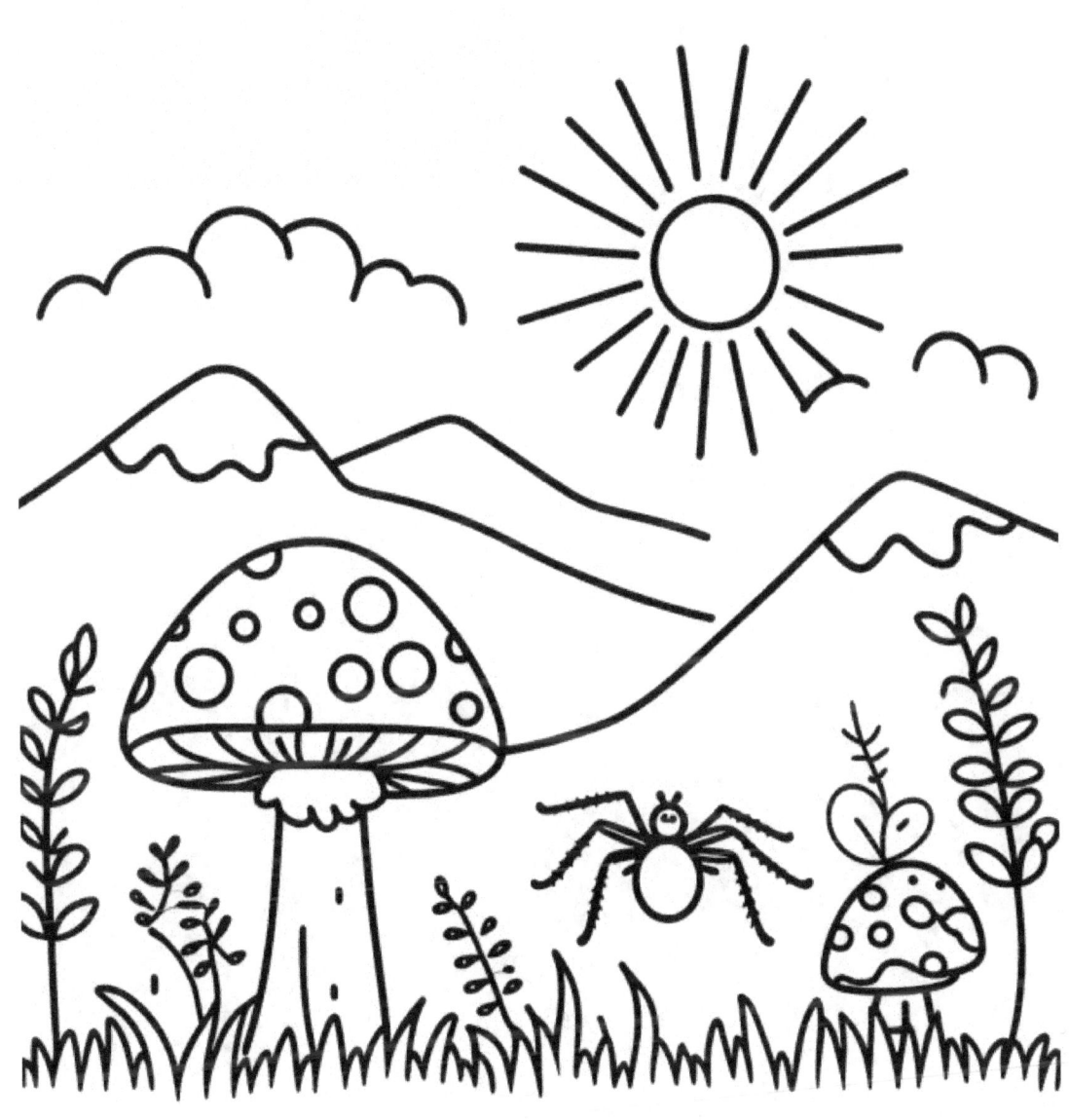

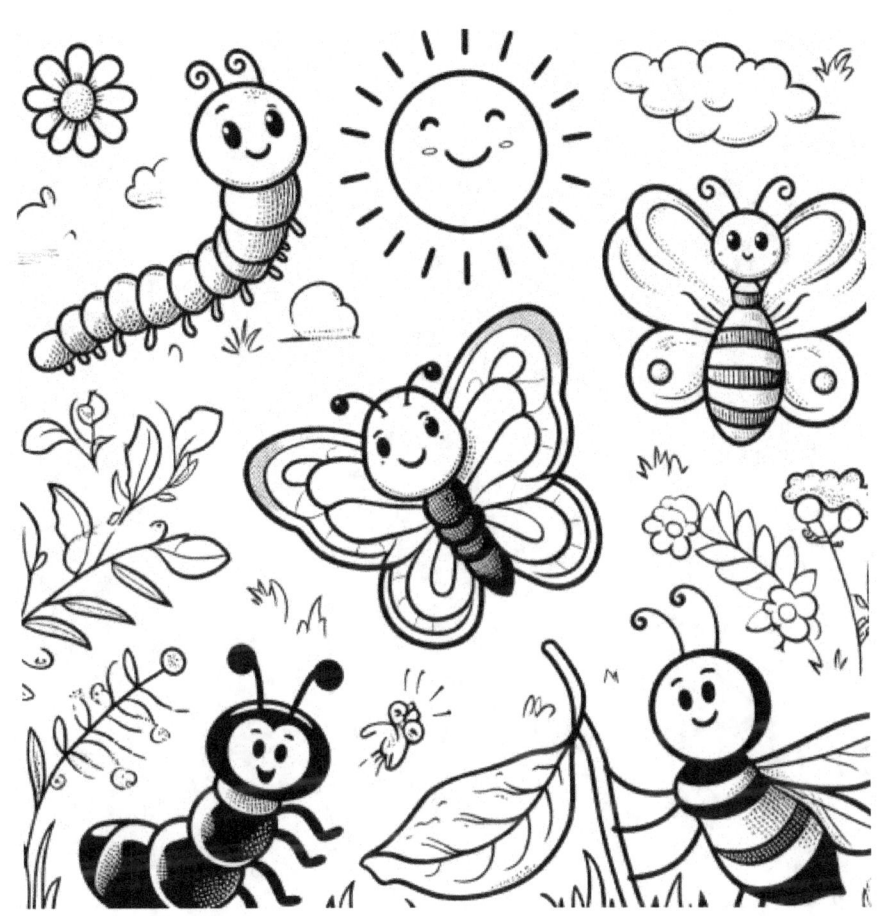

Dear Reader,

Thank you for journeying through the pages of this book

It has been a privilege to share this exploration with you.

If you found the book insightful, inspiring, or uplifting, I would be deeply grateful if you could take a moment to leave a review on Amazon.com. Your feedback helps others discover the book and is immensely valuable to me as an author.

Your support means the world to me, and I am truly grateful for your time and consideration. Thank you for being a part of this journey, and may your path be filled with grace, wisdom, and joy.

Warm regards,

Daniel Adrien Laverdière